India's Bilateral Relations and Foreign Policy

India's Bilateral Relations and Foreign Policy

Edited by

Josukutty C.A.
Assistant Professor and Honorary Director,
Survey Research Centre, Department of Political Science,
University of Kerala

and

J. Prabhash
Department of Political Science and Formerly
Pro-Vice Chancellor and Director,
School of Social Sciences,
University of Kerala

New Century Publications
New Delhi, India

NEW CENTURY PUBLICATIONS
4800 / 24, Bharat Ram Road,
Ansari Road, Daryaganj,
New Delhi - 110 002 (India)

Tel.: 011-2324 7798, 4358 7398, 4101 7798
E-mail: indiatax@vsnl.com • info@newcenturypublications.com
www.newcenturypublications.com

Editorial office:
LG – 7, Aakarshan Bhawan,
4754-57/23, Ansari Road, Daryaganj,
New Delhi – 110 002

Tel.: 011-4356 0919

First Published: **2018**

ISBN: **978-81-7708-448-1**

Published by New Century Publications and printed at Milan Enterprises, New Delhi.

Designs: Patch Creative Unit, New Delhi.

PRINTED IN INDIA

About the Book

Bilateral and regional arrangements have gradually become permanent features of the global foreign policy architecture. India is keen to play a more pronounced role in and with regional and international organizations. Revamping of the foreign policy making establishments is a must to manage regional and international relationships.

India confronts grave security threats emanating from its territorial and maritime borders that range from nuclear attacks to terror strikes. Cyber security threats are a reality today. Are India's defence, nuclear, maritime, terrorism and cyber policies strategic enough to deal with these challenges? Preparations for and views on resorting to the use of force to meet these challenges are of utmost importance.

This book consists of 10 scholarly papers authored by scholars from India and abroad. These papers examine and survey various aspects of India's bilateral and multilateral relations with neighbours, important regions, regional organizations, and big powers. India's response and position on selected global issues are also set forth. The scholars provide valuable insights into the understanding and conduct of India's bilateral relations in the context of its foreign policy formulation.

About the Editors

Dr. Josukutty C.A. is currently Assistant Professor and Honorary Director, Survey Research Centre, Department of Political Science, University of Kerala. He received his M.A. (Political Science), M.Phil and Ph.D. degrees from the University of Kerala. He was a fellow of the Salzburg Global Seminar (2007) and was selected to study at the United States Institute on U.S. foreign policy at the University of Florida, USA in 2010. In 2015, he was awarded the Fulbright Nehru Academic and Professional Excellence Fellowship and taught a semester course on India's foreign policy at the university of South Dakota, Vermillion, USA.

Dr. Josukutty has to his credit 2 books and more than 60 research and popular articles. He has participated and presented papers in a number of national and international conferences and seminars. He has been serving as General Secretary, Association of Political Scientists, Kerala since 2011. His areas of interest and research include international relations, India's foreign policy, Indo-U.S. relations, electoral politics, and human rights.

Professor J. Prabhash presently teaches Political Science at the University of Kerala and is the former Pro-Vice Chancellor (2009-2013) and Director of School of Social Science (2013-2015) of the University. He also worked as Adjunct Professor (2004) at the School of Politics and Economics, Claremont Graduate University, California, U.S. He was Visiting Research Fellow (2010-2013) at New South Wales University, Sydney, Australia. He was Director General (2008-09) of Institute of Parliamentary Affairs, Government of Kerala. He has published 208 research and popular articles and 3 research monographs.

Contents

Contributors

Nayani Melegoda	Professor in International Relations and Head of the Department, University of Colombo, Sri Lanka.
Khadga K.C.	Associate Professor and Co-ordinator, Masters' in International Relations and Diplomacy, Tribhuvan University, Kathmandu, Nepal.
Pradipta Mukherjee	Assistant Professor, Department of Political Science, HMM College for Women, Dakshineswar, Kolkata.
A.K. Pasha	Professor, School of International Studies, Jawaharlal Nehru University (JNU), New Delhi; Formerly Director, Gulf Studies Programme and Chairman, Centre for West Asian Studies, JNU.
Binay Prasad	Research Scholar, Latin American Studies Programme at Centre for Canadian, US and Latin American Studies, School of International Studies, Jawaharlal Nehru University (JNU), New Delhi.
Mathew Sinu Simon	Research Scholar, Department of Political Science, University of Hyderabad, Hyderabad.
K.B. Usha	Assistant Professor, Russian and Central Asian Studies, School of International Studies, Jawaharlal Nehru University (JNU), New Delhi.
Pushpinder Kaur	Assistant Professor, University Institute of Legal Studies, Panjab University, Chandigarh.
Shivani Sharma	Research Scholar, South Asian Studies, Jawaharlal Nehru University (JNU), New Delhi.

Chandrakant Chellany Group Captain CB, Dy. CSO (Air) and Ph.D. Scholar, School of International Studies, Central University of Gujarat, Gandhinagar.

Introduction

By the Editors

Bilateral and regional arrangements have gradually become permanent features of the global foreign policy architecture. There is keen interest in India to play a more pronounced role in and with regional and international organizations. Revamping of the foreign policy making establishment in terms of its strength and size is a must to manage the gargantuan gamut of these myriad relationships. India confronts grave security threats emanating from its territorial and maritime borders that range from nuclear attacks to terror strikes. Cyber security threats are a reality today. Are India's defence, nuclear, maritime, terrorism and cyber policies strategic enough to deal with these challenges? Preparations for and views on resorting to the use of force to meet these challenges are of utmost importance.

This book is a collection of 10 scholarly papers which discuss various aspects and dimensions of India's bilateral relations with other countries in the context of foreign policy formulation.

Nayani Melegoda in the paper *India-Sri Lanka Relations since 2009,* examines how issues of domestic politics could become instruments of foreign policy to enhance relations between two neighbourly countries. India's developmental projects and assistance to war-affected areas in Sri Lanka is testimony to age-old cordial relations between India and Sri Lanka. The partnership helps Sri Lanka to address the question of sustainable development whereas it is critical for India to manage its role as a regional leader in South Asia and gain recognition in a greater international arena. The development partnership is an extension of the natural partnership and functions as the key to closer strategic relationship in the context of changing geopolitical scenario in South Asia.

Khadga K.C. in his paper *Nepal-India Strategic Relations in the 21st Century*, looks at the significance of the geostrategic location of Nepal between India and China and how it has diversified its foreign policy beyond India to balance its sense of insecurity and over dependence on India. He agrees that Nepal-India relationship is determined more by geography and history than by any other consideration. The open border between the two countries is a symbol of trust and friendship. He also agrees with India's apprehension that the growing influence of China in Nepal could undermine India's influence and strategic equations with Nepal.

Pradipta Mukherjee in his paper *India's Strategy Towards Bangladesh: New Dimensions in the 21st Century,* examines major contentious issues such as illegal border crossings, dispute over water sharing, the case of enclaves, migration and question of sovereignty. He emphasises the need for settling these issues amicably. A hegemonic stance by India would have serious impact on the Indo-Bangladesh relations. Application of coercive elements would affect the development of long-term institutional relationships with smaller neighbours of South Asia. He stresses the need for an institutional doctrine to manage India's relationship with smaller and weaker neighbouring states with the aim to give support to their efforts in different segments and secure their support for India's plans for big power status in international politics.

A.K. Pasha in his paper *India and the Gulf Co-operation Council (GCC): Challenges Ahead,* discusses India-GCC relations in a comprehensive manner. He draws out the historical and civilizational relationships between the two regions and analyses them in the context of the changing dynamics of politics in the region. Domestic developments in India have their impact on the relationship. He concludes that the region is becoming increasingly important for India economically, politically and strategically and is critical in India's ambition to become a great power in world politics.

Binay Prasad in his paper *India's Policy in Latin America,* draws out the significance of Latin America in India's plans and projects to become a great power. India's relation with Latin American region has been embedded with myths and jeopardised perceptions. Latin American region, contrary to India's *third worldist* image, recognised and associated itself more with Western Europe than with the countries of Asian or African region. In contemporary times, with the declining influence of US in the region, the space for China and India are quite evident. However, India's chances of making a distinct role for itself in Latin American region would be determined by the tangible benefits that India could provide and not any pre-conceived notions, a mistake committed in the near past.

Mathew Sinu Simon in his paper *India and European Union in the 21st Century,* analyses the strategic and foreign policy orientation of India and EU relationship. He examines the reasons for the missed opportunities and lapses in the relationship. A factual review of the security aspects of strategic cooperation in counter-terrorism, cyber security and anti-piracy operations is attempted in the paper. The author identifies enhanced cooperation in the field of civilian nuclear energy, sustainable development, trade and investment and security-related spheres as the ground for strengthening strategic relations between India and EU.

K.B. Usha in the paper *India-Russia Relations in the Emerging World Order,* examines India-Russia relations in the emerging world order. Russia and India along with other emerging powers represent global transformation from a unipolar world order dominated by the US to a multipolar world characterised by multilaterism and institutional formats such as the BRICS. In the changing scenario, India-Russia relations have undergone qualitative changes. Despite warning by the US, India and Russia have a special and privileged partnership. The author outlines the contours of India's time-tested relationship with Russia and explains why it continues to be a strong pillar in India's foreign policy matrix.

Pushpinder Kaur in her paper *Global Debate on Climate Change and India,* analyses the ongoing debate on climate change and India's position thereof. It looks at how the debate originated and progressed over the period of time at the global level. The paradox of climate change is that the developed countries are responsible for substantive carbon emissions but the developing countries are paying the price for it. Its fallout would be severe on countries like India as majority of people still depend on agriculture for their livelihood. India's response is that the problem of climate change is global in nature and has to be tackled at the national and global level.

Shivani Sharma in the paper *Dynamics of Terrorism in India*, examines how the scourge of terrorism has become a major national security threat for India. The incessant rise of cross-border terrorism and the increased radicalisation of the neighbouring states pose a major security challenge for India. The paper briefly engages in theoretical debate on the concept of terrorism and places it in the present day context of the new wave of terrorism. Reflecting upon the security threat from terrorism, the paper deliberates extensively upon the nature of terrorist threats faced by the Indian state in the context of cross-border terrorism and proxy violence emanating from Pakistan. While tracing the established links between the Pakistani state and the radical insurgent groups, the paper discusses how Pakistani state-sponsored terrorism strains its relations with India. The paper examines the structural weaknesses in India's counter-terrorism policy and make certain recommendations to strengthen the capabilities and institutions to counter the growing menace of terrorism.

Chandrakant Chellany in his paper *Cyber Security in India,* evaluates how India is vulnerable to cyber threats as it aspires to accrue the benefits of cyberspace. While various actors, from individuals to nations, appear keen to benefit from the opportunities afforded by cyber space, they also remain uncertain about its long-term effects. Countries, such as India, require the instruments of cyber space to improve governance delivery and achieve rapid progress. Ironically, these nations also struggle the most in securing their nationals from cyber threats. This paper tries to answer the following questions: Is the danger of cyber security as real and acute as it appears? Is India prepared to mitigate it? Can India guarantee constitutional civil liberties that are now becoming embedded in cyberspace without compromising its security? By engaging these questions, this paper brings the relationship between cyber space and security (of humans and states) to the centre-stage in contemporary debates on domestic politics, international affairs and strategy in India.

We take this opportunity to place on record our deep sense of gratitude and appreciation to all the contributors for their scholarly papers and suggestions to the compendium. Our thanks are also due to New Century Publications, New Delhi, for taking up the publication of this book.

Thiruvananthapuram

Josukutty C.A.
J. Prabhash

1

India-Sri Lanka Relations Since 2009

Nayani Melegoda

Introduction

The main objective of this paper is to discuss India's soft power as an important foreign policy tool by taking up the case study of Sri Lanka-India development partnership since 2009. The two-fold approach investigates first, the humanitarian assistance of India to Sri Lanka ensuring stability in the aftermath of natural and man-made disasters. Stability in the region is an important factor necessary for India's potential economic growth in the region. Another equally important reason for humanitarian assistance in the hour of Sri Lanka's need is the ethnic linkage of the State of Tamil Nadu to Sri Lanka. Next, the development partnership of India-Sri Lanka recognizes the fact that in the last decade or so India has become an "emerging donor". [1]

Significance of India as a donor to Sri Lanka is tied with the importance of Sri Lanka's stability in regional politics. For over 65 years, India and Sri Lanka have enjoyed cordial political, economic, and cultural relations. The hegemonic position India enjoys in South Asia has made these relations that of big power-small power relations. Despite this fact, the relations were never a dependency relationship between the two countries. Unlike, Sri Lanka's state to state relations with other nations, relations with India is also tied with India's soft power that makes a huge impact on socio-cultural life in Sri Lanka going beyond the official conduct of foreign relations. [2]

In the words of the High Commissioner of India in Sri Lanka, H.E. Y.K. Sinha: "India shares a special relationship with Sri Lanka—a relationship that is not merely a friendship but a symbiotic twinning. It is an organic affinity that is not just geographical, but predicated on shared religions, cultural practices, family linkages, linguistic commonalities, economic linkages, political understanding between two democracies, and much more. Suffice it to say that our two countries share a precious and everlasting harmonious understanding cemented by the ideals of great visionaries like Lord Buddha, Emperor Ashoka, Arahat Mahinda, Mahatma Gandhi, Swami Vivekananda and Rabindranath Tagore. The cross- cultural encounters between our two countries have led to cross pollination of ideas, cultures and identities. Anagarika Dharmapala, the great son of Sri Lanka, is one such figure who symbolizes the cultural inter-linkages between India and Sri Lanka". [3]

In 2010, in a joint declaration upon the visit of the Head of State of Sri Lanka, the President of Sri Lanka and the Prime Minister of India agreed that the shared cultural and civilizational heritage of India and Sri Lanka and the extensive people-to-people interaction provided the foundation to build a vibrant and multi-faceted partnership. India-Sri Lanka relations have matured and diversified with the passage of time, encompassing all areas of contemporary relevance, including trade, services and investment, development cooperation, science and technology, culture and education. In consonance with their vision of the future of the India-Sri Lanka relations, the two leaders agreed to further harness the enormous potential available for consolidating and strengthening the bilateral partnership by building on shared values and principles of democracy and pluralism, leveraging common strategic concerns and interests, enhancing connectivity between the two countries, increasing the integration of their economies, and reinforcing the institutional framework for cooperation. [4]

On February 15, 2015, the New President of Sri Lanka made his first official state visit overseas to India. After the regime change, the tense relations that existed in the last few years between Sri Lanka and India has changed to the previous cordial relations, much to the delight of the Sri Lankan public.

India's Humanitarian Assistance to Sri Lanka

According to Global Humanitarian Assistance (Development Initiative), humanitarian assistance is defined as aid and action designed to save lives, alleviate suffering and maintain and protect human dignity during and in the aftermath of man-made crises and natural disasters, as well as to prevent and strengthen preparedness for the occurrence of such situations. What marks it out from other forms of aid and foreign assistance is that it should be guided by the following principles:

- **Humanity**: Saving human lives and alleviating suffering wherever it is found.
- **Impartiality**: Acting solely on the basis of need, without discrimination between or within affected populations.
- **Neutrality**: Acting without favouring any side in an armed conflict or other dispute where such action is carried out.
- **Independence**: The autonomy of humanitarian objectives from the political, economic, military or other objectives that any actor may hold with regard to areas where humanitarian action is being implemented. [5]

The official Organization for Economic Co-operation and Development (OECD) glossary defines humanitarian assistance within the overall definition of official development assistance (ODA), as humanitarian aid and assistance designed to save lives, alleviate suffering and maintain and protect human dignity during and in the aftermath of emergencies. To be classified as humanitarian, aid should be consistent with the humanitarian principles of humanity, impartiality, neutrality and independence. Further, it explains that humanitarian aid includes: disaster prevention and preparedness; the provision of shelter, food, water and sanitation, health services and other items of assistance for the benefit of affected people and to facilitate the return to normal lives and livelihoods; measures to promote and protect the safety, welfare and dignity of civilians and those no longer taking part in hostilities and rehabilitation, reconstruction and transition assistance while the emergency situation persists. [6]

It is said that (Claudia Meier and C.S.R. Murthy) the Indian government uses the terms "humanitarian assistance" or disaster relief" to refer to activities that address human suffering caused by natural disasters. In other words, short-term assistance in the aftermath of disasters is called humanitarian aid. Explaining the religious-cultural values of India, the same authors refer to humanitarianism as a core value of Hinduism and other main religions of India. That is, suffering, selfless nature of giving without an expectation of return, and charity are influences of the spiritual traditions of India. Hence, the Indian decision-makers conceive humanitarian assistance as "extending sympathy" or as a "goodwill gesture" resulting from deep cultural traditions that has existed for centuries in India. [7] Today, India's assistance to its South Asian neighbours has developed from small contributions to sizeable assistance in emergencies.

The humanitarian assistance of India is one hand of India's soft power. Soft power (Nye, 2004) is the ability to get what you want through attraction rather than through coercion or payments. It arises from the attractiveness of a country's culture, political ideals, and policies India's humanitarian assistance to its neighbours is almost or quite attractive due to its Bollywood influence over the region. Therefore, soft power tool is very much within the framework of India's foreign policy today. India's soft power stand as Joseph Nye says, "is an attraction of shared values and the justness and duty of contributing to the achievements of those values". [8] This certainly is true in the case of Sri Lanka since it is one of the top three recipients of Indian humanitarian assistance. Though a small power, Sri Lanka is an important neighbour for India—politically as well as strategically. Sri Lanka came into the limelight of regional politics with Chinese maritime policy and string of pearls strategy.

In providing humanitarian assistance to Sri Lanka, India did not restrict it to natural disasters and emergencies but also provided assistance in the conflict and post-conflict situations

too. First, as a humanitarian intervention, the Indian Air Force flew food and medical supplies to civilians in the Jaffna peninsula in 1987. Next, when the Indian Ocean Tsunami struck Sri Lanka and India on December 26, 2004, it was among the first few countries to disburse aid to Sri Lanka upon the request of the government for emergency aid. India launched "Operation Rainbow" to provide immediate humanitarian assistance to those affected by the Tsunami, in consultation with Sri Lanka. The emergency relief operations of India in Sri Lanka lasted over two and a half months—this remains the largest relief operations undertaken by India outside its territory.

Operating from the Indian High Commission in Colombo, a 24x7 control room was established the same day as Tsunami struck. Within hours of Sri Lanka requesting India for assistance, Indian ships and aircraft arrived with relief material and supplies, and were the first foreign vessels to reach Trincomalee and Galle. A total of 14 Indian Navy and Coast Guard ships were pressed into action. Air support was provided by numerous aircrafts and helicopters of the Indian Air Force and Indian Navy for locating and rescuing survivors, retrieving dead bodies, positioning medical teams and supplies, air dropping food and relief supplies and for situation assessment reconnaissance. Indian relief teams were deployed in many of the affected areas. [9]

India also offered medical assistance to thousands of victims. The first Indian medical team reached Sri Lanka on the day of the Tsunami, and it assisted the Sri Lankan Army in the safe disposal of dead bodies. In addition to medical teams operating from the Indian ships anchored in Galle, mobile medial teams were deployed at various relief camps in remote areas and district hospitals. Indian Army's field ambulance set up medical camps in coordination with the local civil and military health authorities. Specialized disaster relief teams from the Indian armed forces undertook underwater inspection of 17 railway bridges in the southern costal belt and assisted in construction of a 350-foot Bailey bridge in the South East to restore road connectivity.

Indian Navy undertook detailed hydrographic survey of the harbours to provide updated charts of these harbours to the Sri Lankan authorities following changes in the topography of the seabed in affected harbours due to the Tsunami. [10] Next, the focus was on longer term rehabilitation and reconstruction. For this purpose, a delegation of Sri Lankan Parliamentarians visited India to study the disaster management system in India. Sri Lankan officials involved in rehabilitation from Tsunami affected districts visited some of the tsunami affected areas in India in order to gain first-hand knowledge of rehabilitation and reconstruction. Similarly, a team of senior officials from Tamil Nadu visited Sri Lanka and exchanged suggestions and ideas with the Sri Lankan officials.

The Indian humanitarian assistance to Sri Lanka in the aftermath of the 2004 Tsunami is testimony to the close cordial relations the two countries enjoy with each other. By the time in 2014, when the tenth anniversary of the Tsunami was commemorated, India has taken numerous steps since 2004 to enhance its own early warning systems and improve disaster preparedness, where Sri Lanka too would also benefit from the knowledge. [11]

Next, with the end of the war in Sri Lanka in 2009, and in the escalation of violence resulting in internally displaced persons (IDPs) in 2008, the government of Tamil Nadu provided substantial in-kind humanitarian assistance to the International Committee of the Red Cross (ICRC) for their operations in Sri Lanka in 2008 and 2009. The two contributions (worth US$ 2.7 and US$ 3 million respectively) were the only instances where India supported ICRC operations overseas. [12]

According to the table on next page, apart from the Tamil Nadu contribution, and direct contributions to the Sri Lanka government, India provided US$ 2.5 million to the United Nations High Commissioner for Refugees. After the defeat of

Liberation Tigers of Tamil Eelam (LTTE) in 2009, India offered US$ 50 million in medicine and family relief packs (clothes, utensils, food items and personal hygiene items) to IDPs in the North and East. To meet the urgent medical needs of these IDP's, India set up an emergency field hospital in March 2009 which carried over 3,000 surgeries from March to September 2009 and treated over 50,000 IDPs. [13]

In the immediate aftermath of the post-War, Indian attention shifted to rehabilitation and resettlement of the IDPs who accounted for around 300,000. India in consultation and in collaboration with the government of Sri Lanka put in place a programme to provide emergency assistance. This included providing temporary shelters (providing with over one million roofing sheets and 400,000 cement bags) to the IDPs for livelihood restoration. For this, India supplied agricultural implements and seeds packs (95,000). [14] One of the other most important humanitarian assistance was given in the form of seven demining teams (Table 1.1).

Table 1.1: Humanitarian Assistance from India to Sri Lanka: 2005 to 2010

(US$ million)

2010	108	Post-conflict relief and shelter construction
2009	2.8	In-kind to UNHCR
	3	In-kind to the ICRC (Tamil Nadu)
	2	Medical supplies (in-kind)
	Emergency field hospital (treated 50,000 persons)	
2008	2.7	In-kind to the ICRC (from Tamil Nadu)
2005	2.2	Tsunami relief (in-kind)

Source: Meier and Murthy, "India's Growing Involvement in Humanitarian Assistance", 2011, adopted from illustration 4.

Finally, according to Meier and Murthy, humanitarian assistance is explicitly a part of India's aspiration to lead by what is known as soft power. While Indian Bollywood cinema is very popular among the non-Hindi speaking Sri Lankans, India's humanitarian assistance to Sri Lanka over the last decade or so is much appreciated by the public who suffered in the nearly 30 years of conflict.

India's Official Development Assistance (ODA) to Sri Lanka

The concept of India as an emerging donor is not really true in the context of South Asia because India had provided significant economic and military aid to its South Asian neighbours since its Independence. That is even before South-South cooperation (in which India is undoubtedly is a leader) was initiated. Rather than an emerging donor, India has been the top donor to South Asian countries. Yet, India's transition as provider of foreign assistance in a major way can be regarded as an important foreign policy tool to further its own economic, political, and strategic interests. Economist, Dweep Chanana points out that in the recent past, there have been marked shifts in the size, focus and strategic thinking behind India's foreign aid program. In his words, India is an emerging donor on the world stage. Further, he says that India's benevolence is inspired by competition with China which has used aid effectively…through aid [as an instrument of foreign policy] India hopes to build new alliances and further its trade, energy, and political interests…hopes to present the country as powerful and self-reliant. [15]

India's rapid economic growth started around 1991-92. A decade later between 2000-01 and again in 2007-08, India's real gross domestic product (GDP) growth averaged 7.3 percent per annum. Growth rates also hovered around 9 percent and sometimes in excess of 9 percent, except for the period since 2008-09. In that year, the GDP growth fell to 6.7 percent in the face of the global financial crisis. GDP growth rate picked up the following year to 8 percent. The real GDP growth per capita has been in excess of 7 percent per annum for several years. [16] According to World Bank data (2013), India's GDP stood at US$ 1.877 trillion while Sri Lanka's GDP was US$ 67.18 billion. India today, is among the top ten largest economies of the world. This growth has resulted in

India becoming an emerging donor in the new millennium.

On February 28, 2003, in the budget speech of 2003-04, the Indian finance minister at the time announced rather suddenly with great media impact of India's decision to terminate bilateral development aid from 22 donor countries operating in the country. Only six donors were exempted (US, UK, Japan, Germany, Russia and EU) to continue to give ODA to India. At the same time, India also declared that it would intensify its development cooperation with the global South. The Indian Development Initiative (IDI) was then launched. IDI established under the Ministry of Finance was supposed to leverage and promote strategic economic interests abroad. [17]

In 2006, India co-founded the Global Network of Export Import Bank and Development Finance Institutions (G-NEXID). [18] India is also a major contributor to the South Asian Association for Regional Cooperation (SAARC) development fund to promote actions on social, economic and cultural front. India also seeks to use its foreign aid programs as a soft power tool in competing with China for regional supremacy. Hence, India's ODA has been focused primarily on its immediate neighbours. Indian development assistance is used as a foreign and economic policy tool by the Indian government. The goals of India's development work derive directly from Delhi's foreign policy agenda and form part of an overall strategy of Indian South-South co-operation intended to accelerate India's economic and political boom. [19]

According to economist Chanana, there are three main components to India's foreign assistance spending: grants and preferential bilateral loans to governments, contributions to international organizations and financial institutions, and subsidies for preferential bilateral loans provided through the EXIM Bank of India.

Sustainable peace and stability in Sri Lanka is very important to India given its close proximity to the country, and its ethnic linkage with the people of Tamil Nadu. In 2009,

India was one of the first donors with development assistance for this reason. During the long war in Sri Lanka, refugees fled to India. Not only as a big power but also because of the ethnic linkage of Tamil people of Sri Lanka with that of Tamil people in Tamil Nadu, made India monitor the conflict, war and end of war in Sri Lanka very closely. Therefore, development assistance to Sri Lanka was not only an investment for regional stability as a foreign policy tool but also a partnership of long standing. It was also an instrument of extending India's soft power over Sri Lanka and cementing that Sri Lanka remains a close friend of India in the great power game in Asia. In a joint declaration 2010, the Prime Minister of India expressed India's constructive support for the efforts to build peace and reconciliation among all communities in Sri Lanka.

In committing development assistance to Sri Lanka, India is supporting constructively to the object of achieving sustainable peace. India, realized that infrastructure building was foremost important in this exercise. One major project undertaken was the Indian housing project, one of the largest such projects undertaken by India anywhere in the world. In 2010, the Prime Minister of India was apprised of the measures taken by the Government of Sri Lanka to bring about a rapid and sustainable resettlement of the bulk of the IDPs. In this context, India's development assistance was committed to rebuild infrastructure, including railway infrastructure, set up several vocational training centres, repair and construct schools, houses, stadiums and recreational facilities, and supply much-needed inputs for agricultural regeneration. [20]

India-Sri Lanka Development Partnership

Since 2009, one of the most important pillars of India-Sri Lanka diplomatic relations is the development cooperation. India's development partnership with Sri Lanka is tied with India's strategic goal of regional leadership and influence. India's development partnership focuses on trade, infrastructure, health and education.

The India-Sri Lanka Free Trade Agreement (ISFTA) signed in 1998 came into effect in 2000. Since then, India has become an important trading partner for Sri Lanka. India is Sri Lanka's third largest trading partner globally, while Sri Lanka is India's second largest trading partner in the SAARC. It is the number one source of supplies, accounting for 20 percent of Sri Lanka's total exports. Among tourists, Indian visitors make the largest group having a share of 27 percent of total arrivals in Sri Lanka. In the investment field, India is among the top five foreign investors in Sri Lanka. The value of bilateral trade increased from US$ 658 million in 2000 to US$ 3.6 billion in 2013. [21] As per figures of Sri Lanka customs, during the period January to December 2014, it was nearly US$ 4 billion.

The objectives of ISFTA are as under:

1. To promote through the expansion of trade the harmonious development of economic relations between India and Sri Lanka.
2. To provide fair conditions of competition for trade between India and Sri Lanka.
3. In the implementation of this Agreement, the contracting parties shall pay due regard to the principle of reciprocity.
4. To contribute in this way—by the removal of barriers to trade—to the harmonious development and expansion of world trade.

As a result of the ISFTA, Sri Lankan exports to India increased from US$ 55 million in 2001, to US$ 544 million in 2014. Imports have risen from US$ 568 million in 2000 to US$ 3.2 billion during the same period. Though this shows a trade deficit by being internationally competitive, such imports have not only reduced Sri Lanka's overall trade deficit but also provided its people with access to cheaper goods. [22] Currently, both countries are in the process of developing a Comprehensive Economic Partnership Agreement (CEPA).

Next, India's contribution to infrastructure development of post-War Sri Lanka is one of the major partnerships that needs to be stated. This is discussed previously in this paper. In the development partnership of the two countries, one the most important is the Northern Railway Reconstruction project, that connects South with the North. Yaal Devi Express train which stopped its operation to the North in 1990 travelled to Jaffna in October 2014 and to northern most point in the country, Kankasanthurai in January 2015. Earlier, New Delhi helped build the Matara-Colombo railway link in 2012. This is a very important feature in sustainable peace-building efforts in Sri Lanka with people of all communities having easy access to reach any destination in the country. India's partnership through transport projects in Sri Lanka linked the country's North and South after nearly 30 years, a major step in sustainable peace-building.

Agriculture and fisheries are the main income sources for many in Sri Lanka. A Memorandum of Agreement (MOA) between the Indian Council of Agricultural Research (ICAR) and the Sri Lanka Council for Agricultural Research Policy (CARP) facilitates collaborative research and development programmes in areas such as livestock, biotechnology, the design and manufacture of agricultural and farm machinery and equipment, hybrid seed development and post-harvest processing of perishable products, fruits and vegetables. India has also committed to setting up a Faculty of Agriculture at the University of Jaffna in the North.

Development partnership in the energy sector is important for both countries. National Thermal Power Corporation of India and the Ceylon Electricity Board of Sri Lanka established a joint venture in 2011 for building of a 500 MW coal-based thermal power plant at Sampur (Trincomalee) in the East, incorporating environmentally friendly technologies, with the Government of Sri Lanka providing the requisite infrastructure support. An agreement on conducting a feasibility study for the interconnection of the Indian and Sri Lankan electricity grids was signed in 2010. Power purchase agreement, implementation agreement, BOI agreement,

land lease agreement and coal supply agreement were signed on October 7, 2013. [23] When completed, it will be the largest joint venture project between the two countries till date. Another related project of the development partnership is the project to link the electricity grids of India and Sri Lanka. The grid link will help ensure that any excess demand on either side—seasonal or otherwise—can be met by purchasing electricity from the other side. [24]

The tense moments in Sri Lanka-India development partnership since 2009 occurred when the United Nations Human Rights Council (UNHRC), promoted by the US, adopted a resolution "promoting reconciliation and accountability in Sri Lanka" at its 19th regular session. The resolution states:

"Reaffirming that States must ensure that any measure taken to combat terrorism complies with their obligations under international law, in particular international human rights, refugee and humanitarian law, as applicable...taking note of the report of the lessons learnt and Reconciliation Commission of Sri Lanka and its findings and recommendations, and acknowledging its possible contribution to the process of national reconciliation in Sri Lanka".

Welcoming the constructive recommendations contained in the Commission's report which included the need to credibly investigate widespread allegations of extrajudicial killings and enforced disappearances, demilitarizing the north of Sri Lanka, implementing impartial land dispute resolution mechanisms, re-evaluating detention policies, strengthening formerly independent civil institutions, reaching a political settlement on the devolution of power to the provinces, promoting and protecting the right of freedom of expression for all and enact rule of law reforms...noting with concern that the report does not adequately address serious allegations of violations of international law (A/HRC/RES/19/2) was adopted on March 22, 2012 with India voting yes and Sri Lanka calling it arbitrary.

At the subsequent resolution in March 2013 at UNHRC on

requests of High Commissioner to undertake a comprehensive investigation into alleged serious human rights violations in Sri Lanka, India abstained from voting, and on March 2014 resolution on reconciliation, accountability and human rights in Sri Lanka, India voted against the adoption. Yet all the 3 resolutions were passed with a majority vote. [25] Sri Lanka's relations with India were strained during this period with the government hinting at India not doing enough to help Sri Lanka at the UNHRC.

Since the end of the war in 2009, an illegal fishing dispute between Tamil Nadu fishermen and Sri Lanka erupted. During the Sri Lankan civil war, the Indian fishing boats faced risks and occasionally, live fire from Sri Lankan Navy gunboats but were able to operate freely and with little competition, since Sri Lanka's fishing fleet was often grounded during the conflict and war. Since 2009 however, Sri Lankan fishermen have returned to sea and have continuously complained of poaching and over fishing by Indian fishermen—also especially the extensive Indian use of bottom trawlers and monofilament nylon nets by the Indian fishermen that are banned in Sri Lanka.

Unfortunately, for Sri Lanka, the Sri Lankan Navy had on occasions shot these fishermen whereas under normal circumstances these fishermen were arrested and thrown in jail. A Joint Statement was issued on Fishing Arrangements of October 2008, which sought to put in place practical arrangements to deal with bonafide fishermen crossing the International Maritime Boundary Line (IMBL). A joint working group was set up but the meetings were so infrequent and they last met in 2012.

This fishing dispute became more complicated by the issue of Kachchativu: a barren island that lies about 15 miles North-East of Rameshwaran and approximately 14 miles South-West of Delft Islands. There are no permanent inhabitants or any permanent structures on the Island other than a Roman Catholic Church, administered by the Bishop of Jaffna as part

of his Diocese. What makes the island attractive is the annual Roman Catholic feast to which people of the same faith from both the countries participate. India ceded Kachchativu to Sri Lanka in 1974 based on a conditional agreement. Kachchativu is not a dispute between the central governments of India and Sri Lanka. India recognizes Sri Lanka's sovereignty over the island per the 1974 Accord.

As a follow up to this process, an Agreement between Sri Lanka and India on the maritime boundary between the two countries in the Gulf of Mannar and the Bay of Bengal and related matters was signed in 1976. It is the politicians in Tamil Nadu, in the background of the fishing dispute who took up the Kachchativu issue. It must be kept in mind that due to this fishing dispute and straining of relations between India and Sri Lanka, the affected population is the poor fishermen on both the sides. Tamil Nadu fishermen, often poor and desperate, regularly cross into Sri Lankan waters and their counterparts in Sri Lanka resent their presence for the same reasons. Therefore, this is an issue in bilateral relations where both countries should view this from a humanitarian aspect rather than from legalities involved.

In the back ground of tense relations during the Rajapaksa government in 2014, Indian High Commissioner Y.K. Sinha stated during a function at the University of Colombo, that his country was saddened by the fact that Sri Lanka has "underappreciated" the Indian Government's economic assistance to this country. [26] This statement was made in the backdrop of Rajapaksa government's pro-China policy which was not endorsed by the general public in Sri Lanka which firmly believes in Sri Lanka's non-aligned foreign policy. That is, in the context of this paper, not aligned with China nor with India. Therefore, rejecting the family democracy, majority in Sri Lanka voted Rajapaksa out of government in the Presidential elections of January 2015.

Health sector is also a key area of India's development partnership with Sri Lanka. Construction of hospitals and supply of high-value equipment have been the main priorities in the post-War era. Since 2009, there are projects to construct hospitals in Vavuniya (200 bed ward complex) and 150 bed base hospital in Dickoya, Hatton.

Finally, considering education as a key to progress, India's development partnership since 2009 has focused on infrastructure of schools and laboratories, training of educators and granting of local and foreign scholarships. The External Affairs Minister of India during his visit to Sri Lanka in January 2012 announced a substantial expansion in the scholarships offered by the Government of India. A memorandum of understanding between the High Commission of India and the University of Colombo was signed in July 2011 to establish a Centre for Contemporary Indian Studies. The aim of the Centre is to deepen the understanding of India amongst Sri Lankans and to emerge as a premier resource centre and academic hub for studies on contemporary India.

Conclusion

India-Sri Lanka development partnership since 2009 is a testimony to the cordial relations between the two countries in the post-War Sri Lanka. With the change of government in Sri Lanka on January 8, 2015, a regime change took place in Sri Lanka. *The Hindustan Times* reported on January 9, 2015, that five things [in Sri Lanka] would change for better relations with India. Better relations with Tamil people, reducing security engagement with China, smoother execution of Indian development projects in Sri Lanka, stronger trade ties, and finally a genuine democracy. The High Commissioner of India in Sri Lanka called the change "exhilarating renewal of democracy". The new President of Sri Lanka announced that his first visit overseas would be to India in February 2015.

The Indian government is fully aware that recognition for India in a greater international arena depends on how it manages its role as a regional leader in South Asia. Therefore, development partnership is a key to closer strategic relations.

For Sri Lankan people, India had always been Sri Lanka's closest ally and friend. It is natural that the key development partner of Sri Lanka from South Asia should be India. With its non-aligned foreign policy as the backbone, Sri Lanka will take its foreign policy decisions by interacting with two big powers in Asia, namely India and China.

Endnotes

1. Ahmad, Tariq (2015), "Regulation of Foreign Aid: India", Global Legal Research Centre LL, File No. 2011-006054, The Law Library of Congress, The Library of Congress, pp. 139-143.
2. Soft power cultivated through varieties of politics, qualities, action endear nation to other nations, more indirect, non- coercive methods (Neo-liberalism/Constructivism) as opposed to hard power that extracts compliance principally through reliance on tangible power resources (direct coercive methods—realism). The concept of soft power has risen significantly in debates on foreign policy in recent years—also newspapers, television debates on foreign affairs, leading decision-makers especially in the US; Joseph Nye introduced the concept of soft power in 1990, "Bound to Lead" (1990) further applied and developed in (2002), (2003), (2004a), (2004b), and (2007) and Giulion M. Gallarotti (2004), (2010a) and (2010b). Soft power theory has evolved overtime and in world politics, value of soft power relative to hard power has increased. The present emphasis on soft power is a reaction to a large tradition of decision-making that has neglected the benefits of soft power and over relied on hard power. Please see Gallarotti, Giulio M. (2011), "Soft Power: What it is, Why it is important, and the Conditions under which it Can Be Effectively Used", Division II Faculty Publication, Paper 57.
3. Sinha, Y.K. (2015), "Message from H.E. Mr. Y.K. Sinha, High Commissioner of India to Sri Lanka", *Daily Mirror: Daily FT*, January 26.
4. Ministry of Foreign Affairs, Sri Lanka, "Joint Declaration Issued Following the State Visit of H.E. President Mahinda Rajapaksa to India on June 9, 2010".
5. Global Humanitarian Assistance, "Data-guides Defining Humanitarian Aid".
6. OECD, "OECD Glossary".

7. Meier, Claudia and C.S.R. Murthy (2011), "India's Growing Involvement in Humanitarian Assistance", GPPI Research Paper No. 13, pp. 2-39.
8. Futurecasts Online Magazine on "Joseph S. Nye Jr. Soft Power", Vol. 6, No. 9.
9. The Official Government News Portal of Sri Lanka, "Ten Years on from the 2004 Tsunami: Remembering India-Sri Lanka Solidarity".
10. Ibid.
11. Ibid
12. Meier and Murthy, "India's Growing Involvement in Humanitarian Assistance".
13. High Commission of India in Sri Lanka, "India and Sri Lanka: A Partnership that Transcends Time", 15.
14. Ibid.
15. Chanana, Dweep (2009), "India as an Emerging Donor", *Economic and Political Weekly,* March 27.
16. Kumar, Rajiv (2015), "A New India Is Rising", *East Asia Forum,* January 3.
17. PTI (2003), "India Development Initiative to Aid Developing Nations: Jalan", *The Times of India*. April 12.
18. Chanana, "India as an Emerging Donor".
19. Jobelius, Matthias (2007), "New Powers for Global Change? Challenges for the International Development Cooperation: The Case of India", FES Briefing Paper 5, March.
20. Ministry of Foreign Affairs, Sri Lanka, "Joint Declaration".
21. Sri Lanka Export Development Board (EDB) (2014), "Indo-Sri Lanka Free Trade Agreement (ISFTA)", April.
22. Economic Alert of Pathfinder Foundation, "Indo-Lanka Economic Partnership: Will it Help Produce Transformative Shift?", *Daily Mirror*.
23. "CEB Urged to Speed up on Sampur Coal Power Plant", *The Island* [Colombo], online edition.
24. High Commission of India in Sri Lanka, "India-Sri Lanka: A Partnership that Transcends", *Time*, 31.
25. Office of the Higher Commissioner for Human Rights, "Human Rights Council Resolutions on Sri Lanka 2012, 2013, 2014".
26. Sunday Times views, "Saddened by Lankan under Appreciation of Indian Aid: High Commissioner Sinha", *The Sunday Times*, September 28.

References

Ahmad, Tariq (2011), "Regulation of Foreign Aid: India", Global Legal Research Centre LL File No. 2011-006054, The Law Library of Congress, The Library of Congress, pp. 139-43.

Chanana, Dweep (2009), "India as an Emerging Donor", *Economic and Political Weekly*, 4.12, March 27.

Economic Alert of Pathfinder Foundation, "Indo-Lanka Economic Partnership: Will it help Produce Transformative Shift?", *Daily Mirror*, 4.

Futurecasts Online Magazine (2004), "Joseph S. Nye Jr. Soft Power", Vol. 6, No. 9.

Gallarotti, Giulio M. (2011), "Soft Power: What it is, Why it's Important, and the Conditions under which it Can Be Effectively Used", Division II Faculty Publication, Paper 57.

High Commission of India in Sri Lanka, "India and Sri Lanka: A Partnership that Transcends Time", pp. 15-31.

Jobelius, Matthias (2007), "New Powers for Global Change? Challenges for the International Development Cooperation: The Case of India", FES Briefing Paper 5, March.

Kumar, Rajiv (2015), "A New India Is Rising", *East Asia Forum,* January 3.

Meier, Claudia and C.S.R. Murthy (2011), "India's Growing Involvement in Humanitarian Assistance", GPPI Research Paper No. 13, pp. 2-39.

Ministry of Foreign Affairs, Sri Lanka (2010), "Joint Declaration Issued Following the State Visit of H.E. President Mahinda Rajapaksa to India June 9, 2010".

Office of the Higher Commissioner for Human Rights, "Human Rights Council Resolutions on Sri Lanka: 2012, 2013, 2014".

PTI (2003), "India Development Initiative to Aid Developing Nations: Jalan", *The Times of India*, April 12.

Sinha, Y.K., "Message from H.E. Mr. Y.K. Sinha, High Commissioner of India to Sri Lanka", *Daily Mirror: Daily FT,* 1.

Sri Lanka Export Development Board (EDB) (2014), "Indo-Sri Lanka Free Trade Agreement (ISFTA)", April.

Sunday Times Views (2014), "Saddened by Lankan under Appreciation of Indian Aid: High Commissioner Sinha", *The Sunday Times* [Colombo], September 28.

The Official Government News Portal of Sri Lanka, "Ten Years on from the 2004 Tsunami: Remembering India-Sri Lanka Solidarity".

2

Nepal-India Strategic Relations in the 21st Century

Khadga K.C.

International relations are driven by the politics of powerful nations who perennially strive to maximise their power to achieve their national interests (Goodwin, R.E. and Hans, D.K., 2000). "Power maximisation involves a combination of economic growth, military modernisation and diplomacy. During periods of momentous change, it is often noticed that the status-quoist powers try to prevent others from advancing to a higher level while aspiring powers seek to counter these efforts with all the resources at their disposal" (Donnelly, Jack, 2000).

Ever since the end of the Cold War, the world has been passing through a period of power transition and the centre of gravity of international politics has shifted to Asia because of the economic and military prowess of the two aspiring powers, China and India. In this context, the US, as a status quo power, is perceived to be pursuing a twin policy of diplomacy of cooperation and containment to deal with them. China and India, on the other hand, given their geographic constraints, have been trying to sustain their rise by developing cooperative and friendly relations with their neighbours, as well as cooperating with each other at the global level. But as "they are located in the same region, there is also competition between the two for resources and strategic influence. Nepal is quite known for its geo-strategic location in the lap of the Himalayas" (Nayak, Nihar R., 2014). It is situated at the meeting point of North and South Asia, and between two giant countries—India and China—who have also waged war with each other in the past. During the Cold War era, due to its proximity to both these neighbours, Nepal also drew the attention of global powers. Nepal borders the restive Tibetan region of China and has been hosting a significant number of refugees from Tibet since the Chinese takeover of Tibet. Similarly, because of its open borders with India, both Nepal and India have been encountering multiple security problems; human trafficking, counterfeit currency, etc. Nepal has diversified her foreign policy beyond India to balance India to minimise its sense of insecurity and over dependence on India. This has quite often created a mutual misunderstanding between India and Nepal. India, a very important neighbour of Nepal, occupies special significance in its foreign policy because of the geographic, historical, cultural and economic linkages that spans centuries" (Nayak, 2014).

The Nepal-India relationship is determined more by geography and history than any other considerations. The two countries share an open border and unhindered movement of people. The open border is a symbol of their deep trust and friendship. Articulating India's strategic interests in Nepal, Jawaharlal Nehru in December 1950 opined: "From times immemorial, the Himalayas have provided us with a magnificent frontier...We cannot allow that barrier to be penetrated because it is also the principal barrier to India". It has been noted with some anxiety in India, especially by the wider strategic community, that China has taken deliberate steps to improve its relations with almost all of India's Neighbours—after the improvement in Indo-US relations since 2000 in general—especially with Nepal after the fall of the monarchy. India seems like concerned due to China's growing interest in Nepal (Nayak, Ibid).

The concern in India arises from the hypothesis that the growing Chinese presence in Nepal could undermine both India's influence and its strategic equations with Nepal. The only major power located in the south of Tibet, it can be implied that the military build-up in Tibet is possibly targeted at India. In addition, the Himalayas are strategically important for countries like Nepal and Bhutan. These small states act as partial geographical buffers between India and China separated by hundreds of miles and they are also more dependent on their southern neighbour India for easy access to sea for trade with other countries. Between these two states, Nepal has attracted the greater attention of the external powers (Nayak, Ibid).

Historically, Nepal has remained a strategic location for big powers since the Cold War. It has also always figured prominently in the regional power politics centred on the Himalayan region (Jha, H.B, 2013). In return, Nepal took advantage of major external powers' presence on its territory to counter balance the influences of its two neighbours and also to secure its territorial integrity. Despite that, Nepal's foreign policy has mostly focused on maintaining balance between its two bigger neighbours. From the Nepalese standpoint, engaging both China and the US is important because it can counter balance India's influence in Nepal. Both are permanent members of the United Nations (UN). Being a small state, Nepal believes that these two countries can preserve and protect Nepalese interests (sovereignty and territorial integrity) in case of any external intervention, by exerting pressure through the UN. In case of any aggression from India, which Nepal has occasionally and indirectly hinted as a possibility, these countries can support Nepal in the UN and other international forums.

Shah/Rana Regime

After the British East India Company occupied India, Shah Rulers of Nepal were suspicious of those British India rulers (firangis). Nepal became a nation with Prithivi Narayan Shah, a warrior king and statesman about 240 years ago. India and he wanted Nepal to be the real Hindu state. British missionaries had started coming to Nepal and he did not like that. Prithvi Narayan Shah also wanted to maintain good relationship with the Chinese empire and with the rulers in the south (Upreti, Prem, 1996). After the demise of King Prithvi, palace intrigues and conspiracies started and the British took advantage of the situation. They got permission in 1801 to establish a British residency in Kathmandu. During the expansionary phase of Nepali state, Nepal and British Empire came in conflict, which resulted in Sugauli Treaty of 1816 in which Nepal lost at least one-third of the land existing before that.

After 1816, as the consequences of palace intrigues and conspiracies ensued among different courtiers, taking advantage of feuds among the courtiers, Jung Bahadur Rana in 1846, massacred his rivals. Thereafter, the Rana regime in Nepal made important strategic choices in foreign policy (Uprety, Prem Raj, 1991). They basically followed British appeasing foreign policy by helping British to clamp down the Sepoy Mutiny in 1857, in which Nepali troops fought in Lucknow for the British. And also the Ranas wanted to keep the country under isolation from the outside world.

The Rana rulers from Jang Bahadur to Mohan Shamsher followed the same mantra of appeasing the British. They also allowed the British to recruit Nepalese for their armed forces. Because of this policy, Jang Bahadur Rana was able to get some parts of Western Terai including Banke, Bardiya, Kailali and Kanchanpur which were lost to British East India Company by Nepal during the Anglo-Nepal war that culminated in Sugauli treaty of 1816 (Ibid, 1991).

In 1923, Britain recognized Nepal as an independent and sovereign state. Since then, the British adhered to the 'twin-pillar' foreign policy towards Nepal—support both for a monarch and the Ranas. Though it was a kind of pre-modern state building process, the treaty was also significant in that Nepal was recognized as a Westphalia nation state by virtue of that treaty (Ibid, 1991). Throughout the British rule, Nepal largely ignored her northern neighbour China and admitted the British security umbrella.

Post-1950 Relations

Until India got Independence in 1947, Nepal as a nation-state was under the British security umbrella (Muni, S.D., 1973). Later, when India got Independence on August 15, 1947, 'The Treaty of Peace and Friendship' was signed between India and Nepal on July 31, 1950. "From 1950 onwards, though independent India reiterated her re-origination for Nepal as sovereign and independent state, India emerged as interventionist state in the management of economy, politics and security of Nepal" (Muni, S.D., 1977). Independent India's first Prime Minister Jawaharlal Nehru propounded what was called "Himalayan Frontier Policy" which meant that the Himalayas in the northern part of not only India but of Nepal, Bhutan and Sikkim (which was an independent state then) also were frontiers for India's security as well and breaching of those frontiers could not be tolerated.

Panchayat Regime and Nepal-India Relations

During the 30 years long Panchayati regime, Nepal-India relations underwent several ups and downs. Panchayati rulers tried to reduce the over-dependency of Nepal on India and diversified Nepal's relations with the countries beyond India. Nepal got elected as the non-permanent member of United Nations Security Council twice. Nevertheless, Nepal signed a security treaty with India in 1965 that put India's upper hand in arms supply to Nepal. Bilateral relations during the early days of Panchayat regime really remained bitter after the introduction of party-less Panchayat regime, banning political parties and imprisoning their leaders" (Muni, S.D., 1977). Then, leaders of banned political parties were exiled in India, and India was partly helping them to topple the regime back in Nepal.

Amid this situation, India which wanted consultations with it when Nepal wanted extending relations with the third countries, in the meantime, King Birendra in the aftermath of Bangladesh's liberation from Pakistan in 1971 and absorption of Sikkim to India proposed Nepal as a "Zone of Peace" in 1975 during his coronation. Though it was supported by more than 116 countries of the world, it did not succeed due to the fact that it was not endorsed by the most significant neighbour viz. India. India interpreted that move as an anti-Indian step, aimed at reducing Indian influence in Nepal. The climax of sour bilateral relations culminated during 1988-89 when India imposed economic embargo on Nepal (Dharmadarshani, M.D., 2001).

Post-1990 Scenario

Pro-democracy movements were launched all over the world after the break of Berlin Wall and the Soviet disintegration. India supported the democratic forces in Nepal against the monarchical rule. The prohibited Nepali Congress and left parties' alliance launched popular movement for democracy. After the successful restoration of democracy in Nepal in 1990, Nepal had a multi-party political system with constitutional monarchy.

Since 1990, governments of Nepal and India have endeavoured to track on trade and transit relations, exchange of visits and acceleration of mutual cooperation. But due to Tanakpur Barrage issues, bilateral mistrust again went up at some point. Also, when Nepal and India went for Mahakali Treaty, serious debates surfaced in for and against the treaty in Nepal (Nayak, 2014). Similarly, the double-standard on the part of India in Bhutanese refugee issues and the Nepal's Maoist movement did not help to foster the bilateral relationship.

Post-Monarchy Era

After Nepal was declared a federal republic in 2008, India's influence in Nepal further increased. The 12-point agreement between then seven party alliances and the CPN (Maoist) was signed in India with the help and knowledge of India. After Nepal became a republic, India has shown overt interests even in internal political developments in Nepal. India has been said to be engaged in micro-managing situations in Nepal. This tendency of micro-management has been criticized not only in Nepal but also in India as well. India was criticized for explicit and overt interference in Nepal's internal affairs. Against this backdrop, the recent visit by India's prime minister has given new dimension to relations between Nepal and India. The first official visit by India's prime minister in 17 years has helped to restore Nepal-India relations at the political level. General people and political analysts alike have evaluated these developments very positively.

Nepal-India Relations in IR Perspective

After Independence in 1947, India had been able to create a benign image of peace loving nation believing in peaceful coexistence and Panchasheel in international community. Jawaharlal Nehru was one among the founders of Non-aligned Movement (NAM) that was a group of states that neither liked to adhere to NATO or WARSAW pacts. But in relations with small nations of South Asia especially with what they called Himalayan Nations—Nepal, Bhutan and Sikkim—India had not been so liberal (Narayan, Shriman, 1975).

Though, scholars like S.D. Muni claim that India started adopting perspectives of realism in dealing with small neighbours after Indira Gandhi came to power, realism seems to be the modus operandi in India's treatment of small neighbours like Nepal even right after its Independence(Muni, S.D., 1992). India was not happy with construction of Kodari highway connecting Kathmandu with Tibet, an autonomous region of China. The 1950 treaty of "Peace and Friendship", 1965 treaty about arm purchase, 1954 Koshi Treaty and 1959 Gandak Treaty all seem to have been to India's advantage (Ibid, 1992).

All these treaties seem to have a "Zero Sum" nature where India's gain seems a loss for Nepal (at least in the interpretations of some Nepalese scholars). India in its relations with Nepal seems to have evaluated every development in Nepal from perspective of security of India. Hence, whatever may be the image of India in international community in its dealing with Nepal, India seems to have followed the principle of realism. It becomes evident from the fact that, among the issues while dealing with Nepal, India gives highest priority to security.

In treaties and agreements with Nepal, India does not only focus on relative gains but absolute gains and many diplomatic manoeuvres in Nepal, India seems to have acted on the shadow of power. Gujral doctrine propounded by former prime minister of India, I.K. Gujral argued for non-reciprocal relations with small neighbours in the advantage of small neighbours; it did not succeed due to lack of cooperation from the powerful bureaucracy of India. Newly elected Indian Prime minister Narendra Modi has similarly stated that he would focus on keeping states in neighbourhood high on its priority in diplomacy. His speech in Nepali Parliament which has shown respect for Nepal's sovereignty has indicated some positive developments in that direction.

Looking for Alternative Treaty

The most discussed issue regarding Nepal-India relations is the Peace and Friendship Treaty of 1950. Nepali political leaders feverishly raise the issues related to the treaty but our political parties never do a well organized homework to clearly explain how the treaty has adversely affected Nepal. It happens so because they are superficial as far as exactly scanning the contentious contents of the treaty (except, it is heard that a non-paper draft has been submitted to India). No doubt, the treaty is inherently unequal, signed as it was when a newly independent India was dealing with a decaying, feudal Rana regime on its last legs.

In fact, even in a superficial reading, one can easily observe the principal clause of the treaty that brings Nepal within the parameter of the Indian security umbrella (Article 2), which makes it obligatory on the part of both the governments to inform each other of any serious friction or misunderstanding with any neighbouring state likely to cause any breach in the friendly relations subsisting between the two governments (Muni, S.D., 1992). More importantly, the notable clauses that prove unequal are mentioned not in the main treaty but in the 'letters of exchange' attached with the treaty in the annexes as valid as the treaty itself.

Some of the significant provisions of the letters of exchange that reduce Nepal's choices and manoeuvrability in both security and economic aspects are as follows: "Neither Government shall tolerate any threat to the security of the other by a foreign aggressor. To deal with any such threat, the two Governments shall consult with each other and devise effective countermeasures". And, "Any arms, ammunition or warlike material and equipment necessary for the security of Nepal that the Government of Nepal may import through the territory of India shall be so imported with the assistance and agreement of the Government of India". Nepal can show its liberal stand to resolve the issue of 1950s treaty by focusing on ways to resolve the conflicts by distinguishing 'true conflicts' from by establishing principle of differences or by identifying and classifying common interests that might serve as basis for harmonization.

In this regard, in course of drafting new treaty, sovereign, independent rights of both countries should be strictly adhered to. Therefore, as per the sovereign authority of modern independence nation-state and as per the established concerned international law Article 2 (the two Governments hereby undertake to inform each other of any serious friction or misunderstanding with any neighbouring State likely to cause any breach in the friendly relations subsisting between the two Governments) of 1950 Treaty will no longer need to re-enshrine in the upcoming Treaty.

Similarly, so far as Article 4 (The two Governments agree to appoint consuls-general, consuls, vice-consuls and other consular agents, who shall reside in towns, ports and other places in each other's territory as may be agreed to. Consuls-general, consuls, vice-consuls and consular agents shall be provided exequatur or other valid authorization of their appointment. Such exequatur or authorization is liable to be withdrawn by the country which issued it, if considered necessary. The reasons for the withdrawal shall be indicated wherever possible. The persons mentioned above shall enjoy on a reciprocal basis all the rights, privileges, exemptions and immunities that are accorded to persons of corresponding status of any other State) is concerned, aforementioned provisions are categorically coded in the Vienna Convention on Diplomatic Relations, 1961 to which both Nepal and India are signatories, so necessarily may not reincorporate in the upcoming Treaty.

On Article 5 (The Government of Nepal shall be free to import, from or through the territory of India, arms, ammunition or warlike material and equipment necessary for the security of Nepal. The procedure for giving effect to this arrangement shall be worked out by the two Governments acting in consultation), as Nepal has signed a separate Trade and Transit with India, and being a sovereign independent state, she has inalienable right to import, export and manufacture weaponry stuffs too for her security, the provision of Article 5 may also not be necessary to re-mention in the upcoming Treaty (Peace and Friendship Treaty, 1950).

The provisions of the Article 6 and 7 (Each Government undertakes, in token of the neighbourly friendship between India and Nepal, to give to the nationals of the other, in its territory, national treatment with regard to participation in industrial and economic development of such territory and to the grant of concessions and contracts, relating to such development. The Governments of India and Nepal agree to grant, on a reciprocal basis, to the nationals of one country in the territories of the other the same privileges in the matter of residence, ownership of property, participation in trade and commerce, movement and other privileges of a similar nature) due to the demographic inequality between Nepal and India, be better revised in the changing context. However, due to the provisions of the Articles, the huge masses of both countries have been significantly benefiting so the new provisions should be sought with the serious mutual consensus so that there will be no outbreak of any immediate disenchantment from the people of both the countries.

Even though Article 10 of the Treaty states, "this treaty shall remain in force until it is terminated by either party by giving one year notice", it will be better to mention that the treaty be revised and updated by mutual agreement whenever required in the upcoming Treaty.

Redefine Political and Security Relationship

Situated between two regional powers who aspire to be global players, Nepal can grab the opportunities and become a centre of co-operation between rising China and India. Nepal has to accept the neorealist believe of necessity of bipolar competition for stability because of the competition between India and China. A stable Nepal is in the interest of both countries as it serves their prime concerns—security. The realist perspective is dominant on both neighbours regarding their views on Nepal which always focuses on "security dilemma". Both the neighbours have deep concern on Nepal's internal politics and on the issue of their security.

The growing Chinese economic investment in Nepal, Beijing's rising military aid to Nepal and their interest in some political issues such as federalism have been nightmares for New Delhi. They are in such competitive position in Nepal that one's search for security often leaves its current and potential adversaries insecure. The exercise of realist model can be observed in Indian and Chinese competition in Nepal where any nation that strives for absolute security leaves other absolutely insecure. China has specific objectives in relations with Nepal, i.e. to ensure security of its borders and enhance its influence. For achieving these, it gives aid to Nepal. But, India wants to meet diverse objectives: security as a prime concern and political, economic and other resource related issues.

Nepal wants to chart out a more friendly bilateral relationship based on equal footings. While redefining political and security relationship with India, colonial kind of Indian security mentality should be altered by Nepali side. Reflecting its liberalist nature, Nepal seeks to address the problems for achieve lasting peace and cooperation. Nehruvian Himalayan Frontier Policy which has caused structured dependence over India should be corrected in upcoming treaty. It is clear that India has used economic relations as an effective instrument to further its security interests. We have already seen that the economic relations have been used by India regarding its security interests over Nepal and when that was not possible to influence, it withdrew the economic concessions. So, Nepali policy makers have to be aware with the fact that the convergence and divergence in security interests results in divergence and convergence on economic issues too. It means, Nepal can apply the liberal model to secure economic and social interests with a belief that friction will arise only if there is a conflict with the economic and social interests that governments actually represent over the long-term.

The influences of both neighbours in Nepal will increase if Nepal remains unstable, internally vulnerable, and is incapable to resist foreign interference. Politically and economically vulnerable Nepal may be detrimental to protect the security interests of India and China. Both the neighbours have to accept the fact that Nepal's territorial integrity must be acknowledged for their security. Hence, stability in Nepal has to be a top priority for them and it is possible only by making Nepal economically prosperous. For stability, economy should override the politics in Nepal and both India and China should come forward for economic development of Nepal by investing in hydro-electricity, tourism and other development infrastructures.

Only the trilateral cooperation between India, China and Nepal can be in the interest of the region. Security concern has become a major determinant of Chinese and Indian foreign policy towards Nepal. For the neorealist, a state will cooperate if state security is not placed at risk. Being rational security seeking states, India and China can enter into cooperative arrangements with other states. So, Nepal also has to formulate its foreign policy that can address the interests of these immediate neighbours to fulfil its own national interest. To develop such a policy, all political parties of Nepal have to make a common understanding and perception towards the neighbours.

Co-operation and Connectivity

Throughout the modern history of Nepal, geopolitical concerns defined its regional and international relations. Its economic relations with neighbouring and third countries became hostage of its geo-political limitations. Protection of its sovereignty and territorial integrity always dominated its economic behaviour, putting serious restrains over its uninterrupted economic behaviour (i.e. exports and imports). However, the structural changes in global economic relations after the establishment of World Trade Organization (WTO) gradually encouraged states to put aside their political interest vis-à-vis the economic benefits. Communist China and liberal India have strengthened their economic relations despite their contentious border issues and political differences. Maintaining international relations through effective diplomacy to strengthen its economy would be a wise choice for Nepal, given the economic might of both India and China.

The economic relations between India and Nepal are an ancient phenomenon. Nepal's territory, due to its geographic setting, was used for entre pot trade between Tibet and India. Lhasa's emergence as a kingdom of Tibet in Seventh century AD transformed Kathmandu valley into an intellectual and commercial enroot between India and Central Asia. Rather than being a landlocked country having unprecedented dependency on India, ancient Nepal worked as a bridge between India and China. However, the picture of modern Nepal is different. Widening trade deficit, low amount of foreign direct investment (FDI), industrial development at its infancy, and untapped natural resources are its characteristic features.

Though economic diplomacy has been embraced as a vital

aspect of Nepal's foreign policy since 1990, Nepal still lags behind all the SAARC countries in terms of economic growth. FDI, foreign employment promotion, foreign aid, trade promotion and tourism are considered as the major instruments that Nepal can use to boost its economy. However, proper strategies and priorities are yet to be sketched out.

Over the past few years, number of possible options has been discussed among think-tanks and action-tanks on the possible ways Nepal could opt for its economic prosperity. Some of them include, Nepal being a vibrant bridge connecting India and China, trilateral cooperation in tourism promotion, and hydro-trade among others. HIT (highways, information ways, and transmission ways) term coined by Narendra Modi, prime minister of India during his recent visit highlights on the development of better connectivity, communications and hydropower development. His suggestions on the development of adventure tourism, herbal medicines and organic agro products deserve serious attention. In this context, it is high time to develop certain economic strategies considering the changing global order, international trade regime, regional cooperation, and kindness of immediate neighbours.

Overcoming the buffer mentality and putting diplomatic efforts to bridge the giant economies would greatly help Nepal to redefine its foreign relations. While incorporating highest paying economic strategies, institutional development should go simultaneously. Such institutional development include but not limited to clear allocation of responsibilities to concerned agencies, developing investment friendly policies, ending bureaucratic unpredictability, capacity development of diplomats, negotiation authority for diplomatic missions abroad, and promotion of 'mega diplomacy' which include the role of private sector as well.

Energy and Hydropower

Nepal and India have age-old relations in terms of social,

economic and political aspects. These two countries have diverse areas of mutual benefits such as water resources and hydropower generation. Water and hydropower is the most important natural resource that Nepal possesses. It has been theoretically estimated that about 83,000 MW of hydropower can be generated from the water resources in Nepal and it is said that 44,000 MW can be generated in terms of technical feasibility. Nepal has more than 6,000 rivers and rivulets including three perennial rivers, the Koshi, the Mahakali and the Gandaki.

Despite huge possibility of generating electricity, Nepal has an acute problem of load shedding. There are financial, technological and political causes behind the situation with up to 17 hours of load shedding per day in Nepal. Due to load shedding, the day to day life of people has been very miserable. They have a problem in preparing food and enjoying the means of communication. The students are deprived of studying during their examination hours. The operation of industries is not smooth resulting in the lack of expected profit. Some industries like cements, manure have not been established in Nepal as such industries require greater electricity supply. Nepal is unable to export sufficient industrial goods because of this bottleneck.

For rapid economic growth of Nepal, industrial development is very necessary and the role of electricity is very instrumental for industrial progress in Nepal. Educational sectors like schools and colleges are also affected. The sector of health and communication is also not progressing well due to power cuts in Nepal. Infrastructure for development is not well established and developed in Nepal due to power deficiency.

Not only generating hydropower, the role of water resource is also significant for the irrigation sector. Due to lack of proper irrigation system, Nepal's farming is highly dependent on monsoon rain. However, the monsoon rain is also not reliable. Development of agriculture is development of Nepal because agriculture is the main economy of Nepal. The development process of Nepal should initiate from the agricultural sector and agricultural development is supported highly by irrigation development. There is no shortage of water resources for irrigation in Nepal but the management system should be effective enough in establishing required irrigation projects in Nepal.

India is sixth largest economy (in terms of GDP) in the world. To increase the existing economic growth of India, the sector of industry and agriculture should develop more. And for this development, India is in need of more electricity and irrigation provision. If more electricity and irrigation is managed in India, the economic development can improve further. Realizing the need for more electricity power, India has made a policy of setting up big hydropower stations in its neighbouring countries. It has shown high concern for investing in large hydropower projects in Nepal. It will also help Nepal to get rid of its existing power cuts and it will also facilitate industrial as well as agricultural transformation in Nepal. In this sense, the cooperation and collaboration between Nepal and India is very significant for the mutual benefits of both the countries. Hydropower generation is a backbone for socio-economic transformation of any country. It will help to eradicate problems like unemployment and poverty also.

If the existing water resources of Nepal are utilized well, Nepal and India would benefit immensely in such a way that both the countries could be in a win-win situation. The benefit could make substantial contributions to the socio-economic benefit of both the countries. Hydropower is the key to economic prosperity and stability of both the countries. Hydropower is the sector in which Nepal and India can work jointly for gaining mutual benefits. Both the countries can be enormously benefited with sufficient electricity, irrigation, industrial development and recreational tourism.

Combating load shedding in Nepal is the most urgent

necessity in Nepal. The energy crisis is a major problem faced by the nation today. The effect of the shortage of energy has seriously paralysed all sectors of the economy. Nepal is facing 17 hours per day of load shedding in dry season. With sufficient production of hydropower with the cooperation of India, Nepal can get rid of the existing plight of load shedding confronting many people of Nepal. It can export its surplus power to India and the demand of power in India can also be fulfilled simultaneously. At the moment, India should help Nepal with its investment in hydropower generation. In the long-term, it will help India in its energy crisis situation.

Although Nepal has sufficient water resources, it is unable to generate ample hydropower with large scale power stations due to technological backwardness, capital deficiency, shortage of skilled manpower etc. In this situation, foreign direct investment (FDI) in hydropower generation is highly required (Sharma, Pitamber, 2008). Cooperation of India and other countries is very essential in this sector. As India is closest neighbour, assistance from India is very crucial and this cooperation will also help India to solve its energy crisis problem. But the need of the hour is to create investment friendly environment in Nepal with policy revisions, political consensus and political will and commitment.

In fact, due to lack of investment friendly atmosphere in Nepal, donor countries like India were not interested in investing in Nepal in the past. But now, the environment of investment is more congenial with a better situation of peace and security. If the government of Nepal and all the political parties show more commitment and will, investment from India as well as other countries can be attracted and the socio-economic development of Nepal can be accelerated.

To meet the power needs of the country, power imports from India is the first option. Secondly, Nepal can create an environment for the completion of projects like Pancheshwar. This project is the most viable and cost effective. As the power production in the Pancheshwar project was expected to be pollution free, there was high potential for growth of tourism industry also. If it is done after some years, Nepal will be able to supply necessary electricity for the increasing population of India. The present help of India to Nepal will be a big help to meet its hydropower demand. There have been many water deals like the Koshi Agreement, the Gandak Treaty, Mahakali Treaty between Nepal and India.

If necessary, these deals should be revised to the satisfaction of both the countries. There is a perception that Nepal has been dominated in some major water deals with India. In this context, diplomatic dialogues should be held so that these projects are equally advantageous for both the countries. If required, new water treaties can be made for utilization of water resources in Nepal.

There is a problem of power cut in both the countries, Nepal and India. This problem can be solved with the help of Nepal's water resources and the help of India in utilizing these resources. The resources of Nepal should be mobilized in such a way that both the countries are mutually benefited.

For this, both the countries should sit together, hold necessary discussions and carry out essential homework, planning and deals with effective implementation mechanism and framework.

Border Management and Regulation

Nepal and India share an open border of 1,850 km. in the east, the west and the south. The border, which is unique in its nature, has offered some prospects. However, some inimical elements which take advantage of it not only threaten people to people relation but also create bitterness in state to state relations.

Such elements carry on activities like counter fake currency, smuggling of goods, drugs and small arms, human trafficking etc. Another serious issue is about the security, which both countries are concerned about. Criminal activities via and at the border are challenges for national security of both of the countries. Though security forces from India,

Seema Surakshya Bal and from Nepal, Armed Police Force are deployed to control such menace, they are yet to work efficiently as expected. The governments of India and Nepal are yet to work on an effective and practical regulatory system at border without creating any hurdles for the public.

Effective regulation of the border can further strengthen the relations between India and Nepal. In an initial phase, the governments can at least introduce record keeping system of the people of both the countries who travel back and forth. Another alternative could be constructing at least a motor way along with the border that is easier for the security personnel to make an effective regulation at the border and control trans-border crimes.

Most importantly, is the orientation of security personnel, government officials, people and the leaders of the concerned areas regarding prospects and challenges of open border.

Open border is a special security concern for both India and Nepal. India believes that open border is meant for the nationals of these two countries but many third countries are using it for other purposes such as trafficking of fake Indian currency, terrorist activities and smuggling of goods and arms. Therefore, a regulated border regime is needed to track cross-border movement.

Nepal should prove its sensitivity to Indian security concerns. Dealing with India for 'integrated border management' should incorporate infrastructural development in the border areas, including the construction of cross-border roads which connect with Nepal's main highways.

Keeping liberal conception constant that focuses on state interests rather than state power, Nepal assumes that the primary source of conflict among states is not the struggle for power, but rather than conflict of state interests. So, the latest visit of Indian Prime Minister Narendra Modi has been observed by Nepal as an effort to fulfilling these mutual interests.

Conclusion

Indian PM Modi's recent visit to Nepal has raised the hope to redefine bilateral relations on aforementioned issues. However, the political commitment from both the sides should be reflected in implementation aspect of those signed agreements and projects. As per the realist theory of international relations and geopolitical realities, we do not have choice to change our neighbour so foster relations better what so far we have built. The speeding up of cooperation and increase in FDI from India to Nepal would be the best possible model to enhance our relations.

References

Dharamdasani, M.D. (2001), "India as a Factor in Pakistan-Nepal Relations", in Ramakant, et al., (eds.), 'Contemporary Pakistan: Trends and Issues', Vol. II, Kalinga Publications, Delhi, p. 244.

Donnelly, Jack (2000), "Realism and International Relations", Cambridge University Press.

Goodwin, R.E. and D.K. Hans (2000), "A New Handbook of Political Science", New York: Oxford University Press.

Herbor, C. (2014), "Theory of International Relations and Critical Introduction", New York: Routledge.

Hoffman, Stanley (1995), "The Crisis of Liberal Internationalism", *Foreign Policy,* 98, spring, pp. 159-177.

Jennifer, Sterling-Folker (2002), "Realism and the Constructivist Challenge: Rejecting, Reconstructing, or Rereading", *International Studies Review,* 4, spring, pp. 73-97.

Jha, H.B. (2013), "Nepal-India Cooperation in River Water Management", *Strategic Analysis*, 37:2, pp. 217-230.

Kissinger, Henry (2011), "On China", London: Penguin Books.

Muni, S.D., "India's Foreign Policy: The Democracy Dimension", Foundation Books, New Delhi, 2009.

—(ed.), "Nepal: An Assertive Monarchy", New Delhi: Chetana Publications, 1977.

—"Foreign Policy of Nepal", Delhi,: National Publication House, 1973.

—"Impact of the King on the Foreign Policy of Nepal", Jaipur: University of Rajasthan, 1968.

—"India and Nepal: A Challenging Relationship", Konark, Delhi,

1992.
——"India's Foreign Policy the Democracy Dimension", New Delhi: Cambridge University Press, 2009.
Narayan, Shriman (1975), "India and Nepal: An Exercise in Open Diplomacy", Bombay: Popular Prakashan.
Nayak, Nihar R. (2014), "Strategic Himalayas: Republican Nepal and External Powers", New Delhi: IDSA.
Neuman, Stephanie G. (ed.) (1976), "Small States and Segmented Societies: National Political Integration in a Global Environment", Prayer, New York.
O'Reilly, Brendan P. (2013), "Nepal Claims Strategic Middle Ground", *Asia Times*, July 31.
Onesto, Li (2005), "Dispatches from the People's War in Nepal", Pluto Press, London.
Orton, Anna (2010), "India's Borderland Disputes: China, Pakistan, Bangladesh and Nepal", Epitome Books, New Delhi.
Pitamber Sharma (2008), "Unravelling the Mosaic", Kathmandu: Himal Books.
Rasgotra, M. (2011), "Contemporary China and the World", New Delhi: Observer Research.
Raya, Mohan C. Et al. (2014), "Rebalance and Reform", New Delhi: Observer Foundation.
Roth, D. and L. Vincent (ed.) (2013), "Controlling the Water Matching Technology and Institutions in Irrigation Management in India and Nepal", New Delhi: Oxford.
Slaughter, Anne-Marie (2011), "International Relations: Principal Theories" in R. Wolfrum (ed.) 'Max Planck Encyclopaedia of Public International Law', Oxford University Press.
Slaughter, Anne-Marie (1995), "Liberal International Relations: Theory and International Economic Law", *American University International Law Review*, 10, No. 2, pp. 717-743.
Tiwari, Chitra Kumar (1986), "Indian Northern Security and the Himalayan States", *Asian Profile*, Vol. 14, No. 5, August.
Upreti, Prem (1996), "Treaties between Nepal and Her Neighbours", *Tribhuvan University Journal, of Political Science*, Vol. XIX, June.
Uprety, Prem Raj (1991), "Nepal and South Asian Regional Security", *Contributions to Nepalese Studies*, Kathmandu: CNAS Tribhuvan University, Vol. 18, No. 1, January.

Williams, Michael C. (2004), "Why Ideas Matter in International Relations: Hans Morgenthau, Classical Realism, and the Moral Construction of Power Politics", *International Organization,* 58 autumn, pp. 633-665.

3

India's Strategy towards Bangladesh: New Dimensions in the 21st Century

Pradipta Mukherjee

Introduction

It has been one and half decade since India has started the new journey to the old beginning as regards the neighbourhood policy with Bangladesh. Issues like water sharing disputes, illegal migration, border disputes, enclave disputes, transit, insurgency, trade etc. are recognised as the most important areas under discussion in Indian foreign policy strategy with Bangladesh. In the 21st century, the issues remain the same, but they have taken a new dimension.

Some theorists consider that India's extensive foreign policy strategy towards Bangladesh triggers a shift from *moral politik* to *real politik.* One can understand that under the contemporary international order and regional importance, India's policies towards Bangladesh are best understood within the framework of its overall foreign policy concerns. India's growing global presence and its superior economic interests are bringing a subtle reconsideration of its policies towards Bangladesh. With economic integration and energy self-sufficiency emerging as the two most important pillars of its foreign policy, India has made strong economic overtures in the region. Underlying India's current foreign policy strategy is a set of important transitions in India's world view (Raja Mohan, 2006). It is argued that India's attempts at development cooperation in the neighbourhood and encouraging bilateral trade are driven, not just by economic concerns, but by a sharp realization that its political capital in the neighbourhood is fast deteriorating.

Bangladesh maintained cordial relations with India during 1972-1975. The bloody military coup of 1975 killed Mujib which totally changed the course of cordial bilateral relations and advanced 'seeds of discord' and, to every extent, mistrust in Bangladesh-India relations (Bharadwaj, 2014: 1-2). Both the countries are motivated by the shared values of democracy, secularism and social justice. India has become increasingly concerned about Bangladesh, its declining stability and state capacity, and the rising Islamist forces there over the past decades and more. The end of martial law in Bangladesh in 2009 elections and ushering in a democratic government led by Awami League opened up a window of opportunity for both sides to address issues of genuine mutual concern in a purposeful and focused manner that builds in our commonalities (Tharoor, 2012: 100).

Bangladesh has enormous interests about the perspectives and strategies of the new Indian government led by Prime Minister Narendra Modi. Quite rightly so, the current Bangladesh government has worked with India's Dr. Manmohan Singh administration in its last term when both Dhaka and New Delhi went an extra mile to reduce gaps and embark upon new and bold initiatives to strengthen bilateral relations.

External Affairs Minister Sushma Swaraj's first stand-alone visit has set the tone for India's relations with Bangladesh under the National Democratic Alliance (NDA) regime (Pattanaik, Smruti S., 2014). This forms part of the Prime Minister Narendra Modi's focus on the neighbourhood. While the visit was proposed as a goodwill visit, some of the issues that have been bedevilling bilateral relations came up for discussion, particularly, from the Bangladesh side, the conclusion of Teesta and the ratification of the Land Boundary Agreement (LBA), as well as the border issues.

In this backdrop, this paper will seek to understand three specific issues of India's foreign policy strategy towards

Bangladesh, i.e. the issue of enclaves, the issue of water and the issue of illegal border crossing.

The Issue of Enclaves

That people would continue to ignore borders, it is not hard to imagine how often and common it would be for the borderlanders of Bangladesh and India to ignore borders. Historically, these dwellers are not used to geopolitical boundaries and it is only a recent phenomenon for them to be compelled to restrict themselves within a border. Although this border divides a population that speaks the same language and has almost the same traditions, over the sixty years, the border was only surveyed and marked with stones (Baud and Schendel, 1997: 1-2).

The demarcation of Bengal borderland was neither a well-planned job nor it was done by discussing or informing the borderlanders. So it was not surprising that the inhabitants did not, perhaps could not realize the significance of a newly created international border. Violating the border for different purposes remained a very common phenomenon which is still the same in the enclaves of Bangladesh and India.

A Protocol (referred to as the 2011 Protocol) to the 1974 LBA , signed on September 6, 2011 during the visit of the Prime Minister to Bangladesh, paves the way for settlement of the outstanding land boundary issues between the two countries (LBA, 2011: 1-2). This historic agreement will contribute to a stable and peaceful boundary and create an environment conducive to enhanced bilateral cooperation. It will result in better management and coordination of the border and strengthen our ability to deal with smuggling, illegal activities and other trans-border crimes.

Currently, there are 130 Indian Chitmahals (enclaves) in Bangladesh (covering an area of about 20,957.07 acres). On the other hand, there are 95 Bangladesh Chitmahals in Indian territory (covering an area of about 12,289.37 acres, or 4,973.4 hectares). Informal figures tabulated by non-governmental organisation Oxfam, puts the figure of Indian Chitmahal residents at 1.5 lakh people who are citizens of neither country. [1]

The 2011 Protocol will result in a fixed demarcated boundary in all the un-demarcated segments, exchange of 111 Indian enclaves in Bangladesh with 51 Bangladesh enclaves in India and a resolution of all adversely possessed areas. In the exchange of enclaves, India will transfer 111 enclaves with a total area of 17,160.63 acres to Bangladesh, while Bangladesh would transfer 51 enclaves with an area of 7,110.02 acres to India (LBA, 2011: 4-5).

Arun Jaitley and the BJP may have firmly stood against the Land Border Agreement in the Rajya Sabha in 2013, but Prime Minister Narendra Modi has decided to finally operationalise the contentious Land Boundary Agreement with Bangladesh, which may just bring to close a land deal that has been over 40 years in the offing.

After Modi's announcement, a Parliamentary Standing Committee on External Affairs tabled its report in which it recommended that the Constitution Amendment Bill be moved to end the boundary issue between the two nations. Chairman of the panel, Shashi Tharoor, said that the report had been unanimously passed by the Committee, including by members from the Trinamool Congress.

The Standing Committee on enclaves to consider the 119th Amendment Bill to the Constitution, headed by Congress MP Shashi Tharoor felt the difficulties being faced by the people living in the "enclaves" of both the countries would come to an end once the pact comes into force. The Committee are of strong opinion that the Constitution (119th Amendment) Bill, 2013 is in overall national interest as it would pave the way for broader bilateral ties with one of our closest neighbours, [2] Bangladesh, adding that delays in passage of the bill have needlessly contributed to the perpetuation of a huge humanitarian crisis. The Committee asked the government to keep ready a blueprint for development of the enclaves to be handed over to India by Bangladesh so that development work can be started immediately after the pact is ratified.

The India-Bangladesh Land Boundary Agreement bill has implications not only for foreign relations but also for larger questions of human rights, the right to livelihood and even the larger contours of what constitutes foreign policy in India today. The deal would not only end a historical thorn in the bilateral side, it would also open a new era in the relationship. India often suffers a "perception problem" in the eyes of its neighbours, which often view India with suspicion because of its size, economy and military might. That in turn encourages them to turn to China. The land swap deal would go a long way in improving India's local image.

A healthy relationship with Bangladesh would have other economic benefits also. India could seek from Bangladesh as a goodwill gesture, transit rights to its Northeast, bringing development to a struggling region. A deal could also revive the moribund South Asia Growth Quadrangle (SAGQ), comprising India's Northeast, Bangladesh, Nepal and Bhutan. And a deal would give a pre-election boost to the Bangladesh government that has generally been favourable to India.

A land swap agreement would also give citizenship rights to close to 52,000 people: 37,000 on the Bangladesh side and close to 15,000 on the Indian side. These stateless people, often victimized, would finally get rights and privileges as citizens, to the benefit of India's human rights record.

On a broader level, this is an opportunity for India to adopt a new model for the 21st century, one that recognizes the changing nature of diplomacy. As their self-identity grows, India's states and its people want a greater say in how India frames its relations with its neighbours. The land swap deal is an opportunity for India to adopt a new foreign policy discourse that engages the states and the public (Garg, 2013).

Water Issue

It has been argued by many security experts that water shall begin a major source of conflict in the 21st century. The contemporary scenario in India-Bangladesh relations reflects to an extent this dismal truth. Water sharing remains a critical element in shaping India-Bangladesh ties, with the Teesta River dispute and the proposed construction of the Tipaimukh Dam at the centre of the controversy. The 1983 Teesta River Agreement allows India and Bangladesh to share 75 percent of the river water on a 39 and 36 percent basis. [3] But since the Government of West Bengal has a problem on water issue, the Central government could not implement the Agreement as a whole. Now, there is a demand that India should retain 55 percent share of the river's water, while the Bengal government is trying to pursue the Centre for a 75:25 water sharing ratio. But, Dhaka wants equal water sharing of 40:40, while the remaining 20 percent should be set aside for the river to flow.

Fifty four river ways link India and Bangladesh. Being a lower riparian, Bangladesh is keen on signing agreements on water sharing on all the common rivers. So far, there is only one such agreement—the Ganges Water Treaty signed in 1996. It is the sharing of Teesta water which tops the list of water disputes between the two countries and Bangladesh has been insisting on reaching an agreement. In fact, both the countries in principle have agreed on the need for an agreement. But the protest by Paschimbango (erstwhile West Bengal) Chief Minister Mamata Banerjee prevented the signing of a treaty, for which a proposal was mooted during Prime Minister Manmohan Singh's visit to Dhaka in September 2011 (Bhattacharjee, 2013). The Chief Minister objected to the proposed ratio of 50:50 water sharing agreed to in the draft agreement, claiming that the proposed ratio would be disadvantageous to the people of her state. [4] Though, she promised to solve the problem at the earliest during her visit to Bangladesh, in February 2015 (keeping India's national interest and federal order along with West Bengal's interest in mind).

People in the 5,427 villages on the banks of the Teesta are dependent on the river for irrigating their fields and for other livelihoods such as fishing. The villagers, who wage a daily struggle for survival, are the continuing casualty of the India-Bangladesh tensions over sharing of the river waters. During the year 2014, India has released only 10 percent of Teesta's usual dry-season flow, said Mir Sazzad Hossain, member of the Joint Rivers Commission (JRC) in Bangladesh, resulting in the river drying up in Bangladesh.

Under the Teesta Barrage irrigation scheme, Bangladesh needs at least 4,500 cusecs (cubic feet per second) of water for the 60,500 hectares of cropland in the north of the country. However, they are not getting much more than 500 cusecs. The Teesta flood plain covers nearly 14 percent of the total cropped area of Bangladesh and provides direct livelihood opportunities to 9.15 million people in five districts of Rangpur division, according to a study published by the Asia Foundation in March 2013. The Teesta, the fourth largest river shared by India and Bangladesh, also provides livelihood opportunities to 7.3 percent of the total population of Bangladesh. To compound the situation, whatever little water comes is being diverted by the Bangladesh Water Development Board (BWDB) to the irrigation canal of the Teesta barrage, depriving the river and the people living alongside its banks downstream (Roy, 2014).

In 2010, the Teesta water sharing deal made some headway when Prime Minister Sheikh Hasina visited India and signed a joint communiqué with her Indian counterpart Manmohan Singh. Resolving the Teesta issue immediately was part of the communiqué (Pattanaik, 2012). After that, a draft agreement on the Teesta as well as a statement of principles for sharing of river waters in the lean season was prepared. Experts from the two countries reportedly agreed to share the water available at the Gajoldoba barrage in India equally, keeping 20 percent for the river, for an interim 15-year period. [5]

The deal was supposed to be signed during Manmohan Singh's Dhaka visit in September 2011. But it fell through as Mamata Banerjee, the chief minister of India's West Bengal state, pulled out of the deal at the last minute. In November 2011, the West Bengal government asked Indian River expert

Kalyan Rudra to find an acceptable solution to the Teesta water issue. Rudra submitted his report in 2012 in which he said there was a shortage of water in the Teesta as the Indian government had been building many hydropower projects upstream.

In December 2012, Bangladesh and India sought statistics of the Teesta water available at the upper point of the Gajoldoba barrage and Teesta barrage point respectively. The issue has been stalled since. And the villagers are waiting (Roy, ibid). Though we have seen the "saree diplomacy" between Sushma Swaraj and Sheikh Hasina, and the cultural exchange between Mamata Banerjee and Sheikh Hasina, augmentation is doable especially when both the countries are on friendly terms and are willing to go the extra mile to resolve the differences. Considering the federal order, the central Government should think about West Bengal to solve the water dispute problem.

Bangladesh has other issues too. Being a lower riparian, it is concerned over the changes taking place upstream, particularly over the proposal for interlinking of rivers. The Supreme Court of India has directed the government to implement the project, raising new fears in Bangladesh. In 2003, the Indian government had instituted a task force to investigate the viability and other factors of the project. The scheme involves transferring surplus water from the Brahmaputra-Ganga basin and diverting it to rivers in the states of Uttar Pradesh, Rajasthan, Maharashtra, Gujarat, Odisha, Andhra Pradesh, Karnataka and Tamil Nadu through canals.

However, the project could not make any major progress. Bangladesh has been criticizing the project on the ground that if implemented, it would have an adverse impact on its own rivers, agriculture and ecology. Popular opinion in Bangladesh is that India should not take any unilateral decision on the issue without taking due consideration of the needs of the lower riparian section of the rivers. Construction of the Tipaimukh Dam is another contentious issue between India and Bangladesh. Tipaimukh Dam is a hydra power project proposed on the river Barak in Manipur. Bangladesh's objection is that it would have adverse ecological effects in its eastern Sylhet district. In spite of India's reiteration that no dam would be constructed overlooking Bangladesh's objections, the controversy is far from over (Bhattacharjee, ibid).

Bangladesh alleges that India is drawing water from the river unilaterally that has resulted in a grave deficit of the water levels and led to the drying up of the northern districts. On the other hand, Mamata Banerjee accused the Central Government of 'clandestinely' releasing the river water to Bangladesh without seeking their consent. In the absence of an official agreement, technical issues regarding the quantity, division and share of the waters are bound to take centre stage. [6] Though during her 2015 visit to Bangladesh Smt. Banerjee has promised to solve the Teesta issue as soon as possible. At the same time, the formation of the new government is a strategic vantage point that will predict the future of Indo-Bangladesh ties. Despite insubstantial progress, both the Awami League and the UPA governments have maintained peaceful cooperative relations in the past. With the new administration, signing of the Teesta water deal must remain the central priority considering the significant reduction of water levels in the basin and the subsequent exacerbated demand for water in the northern regions of both West Bengal and Bangladesh. [7]

Illegal Border Crossings

Baud and Van Schendel (1997: 211-242) provide some reasons behind these border people crossing the border so frequently, these reasons mainly focus on smuggling and these are: state's restriction on border trades not accepted by the borderlanders; direct results of restriction policies that make certain goods attractive, scarce or expensive; pre-existing networks like kinship, friendship or entrepreneurial partnership; failure of the government to integrate the border economy into the larger national economy; more than a prescribed amount of commodities forbidden to carry; market near the border closer than the mainland; taxation over certain goods (Baud and Schendel, ibid).

Wilson and Donnan categorized three types of border people in terms of ethnic identities and according to them this ethnic identity is one of the major reasons behind crossing border. These are: those which share ethnic ties across the border as well as with those residing at their own state's geographical core; those who are differentiated by cross-border ethnic bonds from other residents of their state; and those who are the member of the national majority in their state and have no ethnic ties across states border (Wilson and Donnan, 1998: 14).

Migration: Question of Sovereignty

Migration and sovereignty have a complex relationship and initial research on linkages concentrated mostly on analysing and assessing the range of possible security threats that could emanate from migration. According to Myron Weiner, there are five broad categories of situations in which immigration comes to be perceived as a threat to the host country, (i) political threat, (ii) security risk to the host country, (iii) cultural threat, (iv) socio-economic problem for the host country and (v) as hostages against the country of origin (Weiner, 1992/93: 103).

Vote bank politics, sheer indifference of state governments often complimented with the inability to look at the bigger picture, the quintessential blame games between the centre and the states on the issue of who is responsible for dealing with foreigners, have all contributed to a large number of illegal immigrants not just settling down in India but contributing immensely to the creation of all kinds of criminal activities. They cover demographic changes, growth of radicalism, particularly Islamic fundamentalism, regionalism, and, more importantly, involvement and even encroachment of foreign powers on the country's sovereign space. All these threats to territorial integrity, core values or socio-political practices of the Indian state interact, sometimes reinforcing each other. This generally leads to the question of sovereignty.

The explosion on October 2, 2014 in a house in the Khagragarh locality of Bardhaman in West Bengal has brought home the worst fears of the Indian intelligence and security agencies. For a few years now, investigators had suspected that after the crackdown on terrorist organisations in Bangladesh, these groups would seek a safe haven in India and, worse, radicalise locals. Their suspicions got confirmed with the death of Bangladeshi nationals Shakil Ahmed and Suvon Mandal in the blast in Bardhaman in which an Indian national, Hasan Saheb, was also critically injured. They had been working on an improvised explosive device. They all belonged to the outfit Jamaat-ul-Mujahideen Bangladesh, or JMB, which the Bangladesh government had banned in 2005.

Officials say several illegal immigrants have entered India through Bangladesh's borders in Assam and West Bengal. They may be posing as Indian nationals. National Investigation Agency (NIA), India's leading anti-terror body, has found that of the 12 accused who are absconding in the Bardhaman case, four are Bangladeshis.

These issues are real concerns for India and it requires a national policy. Absence of a strong national immigration policy is the root of India's inability to deal with this menace. Also enforcement of laws is extremely lenient in India. India therefore not only needs a strong National Immigration and Deportation Act but also require an independent National Immigration and Deportation Agency. Ideally, the agency should be immune from political interference which can only be expected to be extremely high given the vote bank politics and even the money involved in such illegal immigrations. The anti-violence approach with strict policy to deal with illegal immigrants from Bangladesh committing nuisance in India would not jeopardise India's relation with Bangladesh, if there are appropriate measures. Illegal or irregular immigrants overstaying in India and resorting to wicked activities cannot just be treated as a mere law and order issue but is essentially a national security and sovereignty issue.

Data revealed by the UN Department of Economic and Social Affairs (UN-DESA) shows that in 2013, India was home to 3.2 million Bangladeshi residents who had migrated into the country and settled there (Sinha, 2013). The report, released by UN-DESA's population division on September 13, 2013, noted that India has the "single largest bilateral stock of international migrants" in the eastern hemisphere and in the developing world. In 2004, the Congress-led UPA Government came up with a figure of 1,20,53,950 illegal Bangladeshi immigrants living in various parts of India (as per the data provided by Minister of State for Home Affairs on July 14, 2004 in response to an un-starred question in the Rajya Sabha). [8] However, it was clarified by the Ministry 9 days later in the same House that the figures were not reliable. [9] Previously, the BJP-led NDA Government had estimated that there were '15 million Bangladeshi migrants living in India illegally' (Advani, 2003: 10).

In a letter [10] to Principal Secretaries (Home) of all State Governments and Union Territories and Director Generals of Police/Commissioners of Police, all States/Union Territories P.V. Sivaraman, the Director of Ministry of Home Affairs Government of India (Foreigners Division) vested powers to all state Governments/UTs Administrations for *arresting foreign nationals living illegally* in India.

After the emergence of Bangladesh, the Indira-Mujib Pact of 1972 provided that all migrants who had entered India prior to March 25, 1971, the day the Pakistani crackdown on civilians and the Bangladeshi resistance fighters began, would be allowed to remain in the country while the rest would have to return to Bangladesh. Followings are some necessary actions taken by Indian Government to restrain illegal immigration from Bangladesh:

1. Border fences.
2. Laws to detect.
3. Disenfranchise and deport illegal migrants.

4. Identity cards.
5. Forced expulsion drives.
6. Joint border patrolling and other coercive methods etc.

But these initiatives are not effective enough in unsettling the flow of Bangladeshi migrants across the border.

India has a 4,097 km. border with Bangladesh along West Bengal, Assam, Meghalaya and Tripura. Of this, only around 1,500 km. is fenced, leaving a major portion of the border porous and easy for in-migration (Behera, 2011). To regulate the border, India's Border Security Force (BSF), has carried out a shoot to-kill policy—even on unarmed local villagers. The toll has been huge. Over the past 10 years, Indian security forces have killed almost 1,000 people, mostly Bangladeshis, turning the border area into a South Asian killing field. [11] The altercation over the migrants at the border speedily stretched into a full-scale diplomatic row involving the two countries with India forcefully maintaining that the migrants had 'no right to stay in India permanently', while Bangladesh accused India of expelling Bengali-speaking Indian Muslims. [12] The latter strongly denied the presence of undocumented Bangladeshis in India and, at the same time, refused to accept migrants without formal credentials. [13] A representative of the Bangladesh government observed, at a press conference: "how [can] you call them Bangladeshis? Are they carrying Bangladeshi passports or any other identification? There is no question of accepting them" (Kaushik, 2003).

Concluding Observations

Once one said, though Bangladesh is surrounded by Indian border, India still needs to think about Bangladesh. It seems a very hyperrealist question as the easy border access and lack of border control bring various security aspects in the scenario. In the larger framework, the issue of illegal crossing remains a major challenge for both the countries. Rather than dealing with this issue as a problem of trafficking only, the two countries need to take steps to introduce mechanism to deal with this recurring problem of immigration. The land swap will be hugely beneficial for the people residing in these particular enclaves with access to better amenities, services and policing (Sukumaran, 2008).

Regulated border policies and unwillingness to find an early solution to border problems do not augur well for the residents of enclaves. More importantly, the land swap is expected to de-escalate India's border conflict with Bangladesh and help improve overall ties between the two neighbours. Agreement on water sharing should be given priority. Early resolution of the Teesta issue is necessary. The problem could be resolved if arrangements are made to augment the flow during the two-month lean season by storing upstream the surplus water flow during the flood season. It would provide enough water flow in the January-February period, addressing the worries on both sides.

As long as India wishes to continue its relationship with Bangladesh, it needs to take a good glance at the stand it takes towards other South Asian countries also. How far India's handling of some of relevant issues can be called a "success", remains to be seen in the policy priorities of the new government. A hegemonic stance by India would have serious impact on the Indo-Bangladesh relations. Bangladesh-India relations over the years reproduce the prominence of coercive elements in India's hegemonic role in South Asia. This observation will affect the development of long-term institutional relationships with smaller neighbours of South Asia. India should be aware of the fact that Bangladesh's support do count for India's desire for permanent membership to UN Security Council. India's authority in a regional context results in disapproval on the part of weaker states.

Thus, India should rely on an institutional doctrine with bigger association with smaller and weaker neighbouring states with an aim to give support to their efforts to develop themselves in different segments.

Endnotes

1. Retrieved from: www.frontline.in/static/html/fl1912/19120600.htm.
2. For details, follow the report on 'The Constitution (One Hundred and Nineteenth Amendment) Bill, 2013' (December 1, 2014), publish by Lok Sabha Secretariat, Parliament house, New Delhi.
3. Retrieved from: http://www.anantaaspencentre.in/pdf/India_Bangladesh_Report.pdf.
4. "Teesta Deal Uncertain", *The Daily Star*, September 6, 2012.
5. Retrieved from: https://csekarmaconfidence.wordpress.com/2014/08/03/14.
6. Retrieved from: http://www.ipcs.org/article/india/india-bangladesh-relations-significance-of-the-teesta-water-sharing-agreement-4403.html.
7. Ibid.
8. Retrieved from: http://web.mit.edu/cis/www/migration/pubs/rrwp/chandan_nandy_immigrants.pdf.
9. Retrieved from: http://164.100.47.5/newdebate/deb_ndx/202/23072004/11to12.html.
10. Dated, November 5, 2012, retrieved from: http://mha1.nic.in/pdfs/TkActnForgnNsn-271112.pdf.
11. Retrieved from: http://www.theguardian.com/commentisfree/libertycentral/2011/jan/23/india-bangladesh-border-shoot-to-kill-policy.
12. See Hindu (2003), 'They Have no Right to Stay Here: Advani', February 6, and Hindustan Times (2003b), 'Bangladesh Tells India to Stop 'Push-ins' at Border', February 5.
13. See Telegraph (2003), 'Election Heat on Bangla Migrants', January 31.

References

Advani, L.K. (2003), Deputy Prime Minister and Union Home Minister, Government of India, in his statement before the Parliamentary Consultative Committee on Home Affairs, New Delhi.

Baud, M. and Van Schendel, W. (1997), "Toward a Comparative History of Borderlands", *Journal of World History,* 8 (2), 211.

Baud, M. and Van Schendel, W. (1997), "Toward a Comparative History of Borderlands", *Journal of World History,* 8 (2).

Behera, Dr. Subhakanta (2011), "Trans-border Identities: A Study on the Impact of Bangladeshi and Nepali Migration to India", ICRIER Policy Series, No. 1, Page 1. The paper was commissioned under the Strategic and Economic Capacity-building Programme (SECP). The research focus of the SECP is on economic-strategic issues of the future in the context of Asian peace and security.

Bharadwaj, Sanjay (2014), "Policy Options for India in Bangladesh", IPCS, Issue Brief # 251.

Bhattacharjee, Joyeeta (2012), "India-Bangladesh Relations: Finding a Way Forward", ORF Issue Brief #43.

Garg, Sanjeeb Ibu (2013), "The India-Bangladesh Land-Swap Deal", retrieved from: https://thediplomat.com/2013/09/the-india-bangladesh-land-swap-deal.

"India and Bangladesh: Land Boundary Agreement" (2011), Published by Public Diplomacy Division, MEA, GoI.

Kaushik, Narendra (2003), "Bangladesh Turns Back Deported People", *Mid-Day*, January 28.

Myron, Weiner (1992/93), "Security, Stability and International Migration", *International Security*, Vol. 17, No. 3.

Nair, P. Sukumaran (2008), "Indo-Bangladesh Relations", New Delhi, APH Publishing.

Pattanaik, Smruti S. (2012) "Four Decades of India-Bangladesh Relations: Historical Imperatives and Future Direction", New Delhi: Gyan Publishing House.

Pattanaik, Smruti S. (2014), "Sushma Swaraj's Visit to Bangladesh: A New Beginning", IDSA Comment, retrieved from: http://www.idsa.in/idsacomments/sushmaswarajsvisittobangladesh_sspattaniak_300614.html.

Raja Mohan, C. (2006), "India's New Foreign Policy Strategy", Draft paper presented at a Seminar in Beijing by China Reform Forum and the Carnegie Endowment for International Peace, Beijing.

Roy, Pinaki (2014), "Teesta River Runs Dry as India and Bangladesh Fail to Resolve Disputes", retrieved from: http://www.thethirdpole.net/teesta-river-runs-dry-as-india-and-bangladesh-fail-to-resolve-disputes.

Sinha, Kounteya, TNN (2013), Retrieved from: http://articles.timesofindia.indiatimes.com/2013-09-13/india/42040328_1_bangladeshi-migrants-south-asians-largest-group.

Tharoor, Shashi (2012), "Pax Indica: India and the World of the 21st Century", New Delhi: Penguin Books.

Wilson, T.M. and Donnan, H. (1998), "Border Identities: Nation and State at International Frontiers", Cambridge: Cambridge University Press.

4

India and the Gulf Co-operation Council (GCC) Countries: Challenges Ahead

A.K. Pasha

Introduction:

The Gulf coastal area in which the GCC states are located has since times immemorial been a meeting place for people not only from the neighbourhood but also for people as far away as China. They had a powerful presence in the Indian Ocean region. It was only with the arrival of the Europeans starting with the Portuguese who reached Calicut in 1498 that the supremacy of the Gulf Arabs disappeared soon after except for Omani influence in East Africa. The Europeans due to bigger ships, mounted with heavy guns evicted the Arabs from many port cities all over Asia. The Persian rulers along with the Arabs especially from Oman and Yemen were able to thwart the designs of the Europeans.

The British after defeating Tipu Sultan in 1799 who was the last South Indian ruler to resist the British, used Indian soldiers to dominate the Arab world and soon Arabs saw Indians as collaborators with British imperialism. Many Indian soldiers died suppressing the Arabs who opposed British imperialism. Nehru supported the Palestinians and all Arab freedom movements. India favoured a federal state in Palestine. India had to keep in mind Pakistan's role in working for a Pan-Islamic bloc with the help of UK-USA in the Arab world, along with the Kashmir issue and advocacy of the rights of Indian Muslims. During the early periods, India's relation with this region was influenced by Arab Nationalism led by Nasser of Egypt and Pan-Islamic policy of Saudi Arabia. In early Cold War days, India had a very close relationship with Egypt. Gradually, the Saudis began to play an increasingly important role in the region.

The Saudis took interest in the establishment of the OIC in May 1971. In the light of new regional developments, India had to reorient its policy from one of heavy reliance on Cairo, to other power centres which had emerged in the Gulf area. The Gulf Arabs came to be known in a big way especially after they used [with other Arabs] oil as a political weapon in 1973 to punish Israel, USA and others supporters of the Zionist state. The Arab states due to India's unequivocal support for the Arab and Palestinian causes assured New Delhi, an uninterrupted supply of oil and treated India as a "friend". Thus, India due to its consistent support to the Arab causes was assured of the oil supply. Moreover, India's policy opened significant possibilities for Indian exports. It soon led to a large presence of Indian workers in the Gulf area. Soon India's economic and political contacts widened with the oil rich Arab Gulf States. This partly alleviated India's balance of payment situation caused due to increase in the oil prices. These developments brought India and the Arab Gulf States closer.

The 1979 Revolution in Iran and the outbreak of war between two major NAM members viz. Iran and Iraq (in September 1980) was a cause for deep concern to India. Of particular significance to India was the fact that both were New Delhi's major suppliers of crude oil supplying about 75 percent of Indian oil imports. In addition, many Indians were working in several projects sending remittances. Indian policy makers feared major powers involvement in yet another conflict in the Gulf area where developments related to security and instability had a direct bearing on India's security.

India was strictly neutral but friendly ties with Iraq gave a certain tilt towards Baghdad. The Soviet withdrawal from Afghanistan and the disintegration of USSR in 1991 together with the end of the Cold War and the emergence of Pax Americana in the Arab world initiated a gradual but necessary change in India's policy towards the Arab world while at the same time continuing its basic policy. It can be seen as realistic as well as practical in terms of its objectives. In the wake of the 1990-91 Kuwait crisis and the Madrid Peace Conference [October 1991], India decided to establish full diplomatic ties with Israel on January 29, 1992. Things changed dramatically after 1991 when both Arabs and Israelis decided to negotiate their problems.

GCC and the Babri Masjid Issue

In India, BJP leader Mr. L.K. Advani in 1991 led protest movement from Somnath in Gujarat to Ayodhya in UP, which culminated in the destruction of the Babri Masjid. The GCC on December 6, 1992 at the 13th summit in Abu Dhabi [UAE] described the Babri Mosque destruction by the BJP and its ideological allies as "sacrilege and an unpardonable act". The Council adopted a resolution titled "Aggression against the Babri Masjid" in which it expressed its "deep condemnation of the Babri Masjid demolition" which was described as a "crime against Muslim holy places". The resolution called upon the Indian government to uphold its responsibilities and to take further measures to protect the Indian Muslims, their religious rights and places of worship.

India and the UAE

Among all the GCC states, India enjoys the strongest economic and political relationship with the UAE since its independence on December 2, 1971. India's trade [exports] and import of oil and the presence of Indian workers in UAE is economically very significant. UAE was the first GCC State to provide aid to India through Abu Dhabi Fund for Economic Development [ADFAED] for India's infrastructure projects. Reputed Indian companies like the Tatas, Kamanis, Dastur and others have taken part in the industrial development of UAE. In the Jebel Ali free trade zone, over 160 Indian companies—the largest number from any one country—have taken part, including joint ventures.

The stand adopted by the UAE on Kashmir at all meetings until recently had been remarkably restrained. But since the 1992 Babri Masjid event and Bombay bomb blasts, the UAE appears to have shifted from its earlier position. At the OIC foreign ministers at Karachi in 1994, the UAE called for guaranteeing the "national rights and the Islamic identity of Kashmiri people". The UAE condemned all sorts of terrorism and violence which resulted in the killing of innocent people. It agreed to work with India to curb terrorism and step up cooperation in security measures.

India and Kuwait

Kuwait had expressed its deep disappointment over India's pro-Iraqi position on the occupation of the Emirate. Not surprisingly, Kuwait, at a number of the Organization of Islamic Conference (OIC) meetings after the war, had launched a scathing attack against India and had supported Pakistan's stand on holding a plebiscite in Kashmir. Even though ties between India and the GCC states improved gradually, the Kashmir and Ayodhya issues continued to bedevil relations to some extent even now. Kuwait's Foreign Minister expressed the hope that India would rebuild the Babri Masjid and hand it over to the Indian Muslims. Also in protest against the demolition of the Babri Masjid, a proposal was tabled by two Kuwaiti independent MPs, Mr. Khalid al Adwah [an Islamist] and Mr. Mohammed Sharar, in the Kuwaiti National Assembly, in January 1994 for boycott of Indian Hindu workers and a ban on their entry and recruitment into Kuwait. The Kuwaiti government on August 15, 1994 rejected the proposal saying that such a move would worsen Kuwait's relations with "friendly India" and stressed that the proposal violated political and religious norms.

Despite Kuwaiti unhappiness, India accepted membership of the 35-nation United Nations Iraq-Kuwaiti Observer Mission [UNIKOM] to patrol the Demilitarized Zone [DMZ] along the Iraq-Kuwait border. India was also associated in the monitoring commissions and teams meant to supervise Iraqi payment of compensation and elimination of WMD. India's External Affairs Minister Madhavsinh Solanki visited Kuwait in mid-February 1992—the first ministerial visit to Kuwait since the 1990-91 Iraq-Kuwait war. The visit was primarily aimed at building bridges with Kuwait after India's ambivalent attitude during its occupation by Iraq. As seen earlier, relations between the two had deteriorated and Kuwaiti leaders publicly expressed anguish and surprise at India's stand during the Kuwaiti crisis. After the talks with the Kuwaiti leaders, Mr. Solanki said, Kuwait wanted India and Pakistan to resolve the Kashmir issue through peaceful negotiations in accordance with international norms.

Also, Kuwait Fund for Arab Economic Development [KFAED] has been giving economic aid to India on low interest rate since it started in 1975-76. The Fund has tried to limit the impact of political considerations on its lending operations. Most of the studies regarding operations offered, have noted lack of discrimination on political grounds in loan disbursements. In the aftermath of the Gulf war, India through its skilful diplomacy succeeded in clearing the misunderstanding with the GCC States and in particular with Kuwait. Despite Kuwait's unhappiness over India's ambiguous position during Iraq's invasion, a number of Indian firms were given contracts in the rebuilding of Kuwait.

India and Saudi Arabia

King Saud Bin Abdul Aziz of Saudi Arabia paid a visit to India in November-December 1955. On December 10, 1955, he told the Indo-Arab Society in Bombay, "I desire to say to my Muslim brethren all over the world with satisfaction that the fate of the Indian Muslims is in safe hands. In my capacity as the guardian of Muslim holy places, I desire to express my gratitude to the great Indian leader, Mr. Nehru, and all those lieutenants of his, through whom he executes this policy of equality and equity". A joint statement said that both countries are resolved to strengthen the existing friendly ties through further cooperation to their mutual advantage in the cultural, political and economic spheres. When India's Prime Minister Jawaharlal Nehru returned the visit in September 1956, he was given a rousing welcome with slogans of "Welcome Prophet of Peace" which obviously angered many in the Islamic world including in Pakistan.

However, in the aftermath of the 1956 Suez crisis, US influence on the Kingdom increased, with Riyadh accepting the Eisenhower Doctrine directed at Egypt and USSR. Soon Riyadh-Pakistan ties became closer, with the result that a Saudi-Pakistan alliance virtually came to be established in mid-1960s with Riyadh terming India as an aggressor in the Indo-Pak war of 1965 and warned India not to take advantage of its close ties with the Arab and Islamic states. This was mainly due to close Indo-Egyptian friendship and Nasser's support to Indian position at several forums. The Bangladesh crisis and the Indo-Pak war of 1971 had a major impact on Indo-Saudi ties. Riyadh's position on the crisis at the UN was that the developments in East Pakistan were Islamabad's internal affair and that no other country had any right to interfere in the same.

However, India managed to convince the Saudi rulers of New Delhi's sincere desire to live in peace with Pakistan and respect its territorial integrity. The 1972 Shimla Pact and the release of Pakistani prisoners by India helped the atmosphere, as Saudi concerns for Pakistani territorial integrity had become an issue in India's bilateral ties. The 1979 Iranian revolution, Soviet intervention in Afghanistan and the Iran-Iraq War [1980-88] brought about closer Saudi-Pak ties. But Saudi military aid to Pakistan became a major irritant in relations between New Delhi and Riyadh.

It is in this backdrop one should see Mrs. Indira Gandhi's visit to Riyadh in April 1982 which ended the 26 years long communication gap between the two states. Her visit paved the way for better relations and heralded a new era. Since the emergence of militancy in Kashmir in 1989 and the demolition of Babri Masjid in 1992, India worked hard to improve ties with the Kingdom. The opportunity to cement that effort came following 9/11, when Saudi Arabia responded to Indian overtures, realizing that both countries face the common scourge of terrorism. Since then, Riyadh has condemned all forms of extremism and terrorism, including the attack on Indian Parliament in 2001.

In a major breakthrough, India received Saudi King Abdullah on January 26, 2006 as the chief guest at the Republic Day celebrations in New Delhi. He became the first Saudi king to get that honour. The tradition of inviting a head of state as chief guest at the Republic Day parade every year is now considered a measure of importance India attaches to that country, apart from serving as an opportunity to showcase the country's military might as well as secular and democratic traditions. For the last half century, no Saudi ruler has visited India as the Kingdom enjoyed close ties with Pakistan. Since the Babri Masjid issue (1992) and the Kashmir issue (militancy), India had been working hard to improve ties with the Kingdom. Also since 9/11, there has been a realization among Saudi circles of the need to improve ties with India. Both the countries have been facing the common challenge of terrorism. Saudi Arabia condemned the 2001 attack on Indian Parliament in New Delhi.

The Kingdom is also appreciative of Indian stand on the Kashmir issue and signalled that its ties with Pakistan need not come in the way of better ties with India. Based on its new diplomacy of promoting cooperation between importers and exporters of crude oil, India and Saudi Arabia are encouraging cross investments in the industry, mining and energy sectors. The two countries signed a memorandum of understanding on meeting challenges such as crime and terrorism. There are over 1.8 million Indian workers gainfully employed in the Kingdom who send valuable remittances in foreign exchange which form a good part of the trade bill for India.

More than one lakh Indian Muslims go on Haj pilgrimage annually to the Kingdom besides several thousand making the

Umra—lesser pilgrimage every year. The visit of the King gives a big boost to the tourist traffic between the two countries with Saudi visitor arrivals in India increasing every year. The figures are rising as Saudis discover India as a viable destination for medical treatment, education and sight-seeing. The official international carrier, Air India, now generates over 20 percent of its revenue from the Gulf, with the Saudi sector accounting for 30 percent of the figure. Clearly, relations are likely to see an upswing in the coming years.

In the broader context of rapidly improving Indo-US ties, closer Indo-Saudi ties are likely to be upgraded which could include security cooperation to meet common challenges. King Abdullah's visit should kick-start a process that will look beyond religion, oil and employment, as well as remain independent of its close ties with Pakistan. Prime Minister Dr. Manmohan Singh returned the visit in 2010 where he signed several agreements with Riyadh. The Indian PM Modi's visit in 2016 was a landmark in the Indo-Saudi relationship. Both the countries have entered into a number of agreements including the fight against terrorism.

Ties with Bahrain, Qatar and Oman

In a smaller or larger measure, Bahrain, Qatar and Oman have either expressed disinterest or toned down their earlier stance on Kashmir. Bahrain is now allowing Indians with more than 15 years experience and a healthy bank balance to reside in the country even without work permits. Bahrain's PM Sheikh Khalifa bin Salman Al Khalifa's visit in January 2004—the first to India, boosted the cooperation between the two countries. Both signed an extradition treaty, mutual legal assistance and judicial cooperation in civil, criminal and commercial matters, bilateral investment promotion agreement and avoiding double taxation. The ICICI and SBI were given offshore banking unit license and a restricted full commercial bank license. The Electronic and Computer Software Export Promotion Council of India sent a 15-member delegation to

Bahrain in May 2001. They signed a MoU with Bahrain Economic Development Board for development of the IT sector.

Meanwhile, India's asset management company, Unit Trust of India [UTI] is to offer its award winning mutual fund for investors in Bahrain. UTI Int., a 100 percent subsidiary of UTI, opened its representative office in Bahrain in July 2005. The fact that Bahrain has emerged as the financial hub in the GCC has attracted the attention of Indian banks and financial companies. No wonder, ICICI Prudential Life Insurance Company, life insurance subsidiary of ICICI Bank, India's second largest bank, is to open its first overseas office in Bahrain. The company has received approval from the Bahrain Monetary Agency [BMA] to open its representative office. In addition, ICICI Bank has established a tie-up with Bahrain Financing Company [BFC], the first foreign exchange company in the island Kingdom.

To keep up with the growing volume of air traffic, Air India Express, India's first international budget airline has extended its operations to Bahrain from Kochi, Mumbai and New Delhi. Already, such service operates to Muscat and Abu Dhabi and other Gulf cities.

India and Oman

India has historic ties with Oman dating back to the Indus Valley civilization with archaeological findings indicating regular maritime navigation especially to Omani ports like Sur, Muscat, Qalhat and Qurayyet. After India's Independence both countries signed a Treaty of friendship, commerce and navigation on May 13, 1953 even though diplomatic ties were established in 1955. It is only since 1970 that Oman has been following an independent foreign policy under Sultan Qaboos. During the 1971 Bangladesh crisis, Oman was the only Arab [Muslim] country that did not completely side with Pakistan. The first MoU related to defence cooperation was signed on December 12, 1983 which envisaged deputation of medical personnel to the Omani Ministry of Defence. Starting from the first high level visit by External Affairs Minister Mr. Swaran Singh in January 1973, a large number of Indian leaders have been to Oman. All of these visits over the years have led to the establishment of close political, economic, security and cultural relations.

On the occasion of completion of 50 years of diplomatic ties both organized a number of events to mark this milestone. With the signing of a MoU for the establishment of Oman India Strategic Consultation Group on February 7, 2002, bilateral ties took a new height—especially in the strategic dimension. Indian Prime Minister Manmohan Singh visited Oman in November 2008 and established an India-Oman Joint Investment Fund with a seed capital of US$ 100 million which would be extendable to US$ 1.5 billion. In recent times, Indo-Oman relationship is growing in the field of military cooperation and fighting terrorism.

GCC-India Relations: Regional and Global Factors

After concluding the India-US agreement on nuclear issues on July 18, 2005, India decided for enhanced cooperation with the GCC countries and to work on a free trade agreement with the six nation GCC. With no exception, all the six GCC States have unambiguously indicated that they would be interested in investing in India.

One must remember that all the GCC States have close relations with the US and India's own ties with the US have seen upswing in recent times. India decided to work with individual GCC countries for agreements on the lines of the Singapore one which would cover services and investment. India saw the free trade agreement which will open the gateway to the rest of the Arab countries for Indian business. Despite global search for oil/gas resources, the focus remains on the Gulf region to ensure adequate supplies to sustain its high economic growth.

The GCC region has become an important foreign

exchange earning zone from the standpoint of growing trade, workers' remittances, and investment opportunities and tourism. Gulf region being an extended neighbourhood of the Indian sub-continent, makes India pursue pragmatic policies taking into consideration the sensitivities of the United States, Israel, GCC states and India's own interests.

The economic-commercial content in India-GCC relationship is growing and has more potential to expand for mutual benefit. The new development is that India would be working in tandem with the United States in the GCC region, to further promote its core interests. Major highlights in GCC-India Relations have been the steps that both have taken towards initiating negotiations for a free trade pact.

The proposed GCC-India FTA along with the signing of the Bilateral Investment Promotion and Protection Agreement between India and other GCC states will create more favourable atmosphere for increased GCC investments in India as the current levels are only a pittance compared to what the GCC have invested in Western States.

This is likely to boost trade and commercial ties and allows movement of goods and services for mutual benefit. It is also likely to strengthen eventually the institutional or structural ties between GCC and SAARC.

This may be expanded with the inclusion of Afghanistan. India considers the GCC region as its "natural economic hinterland". The presence of over six million Indian workers in the GCC states is an important link as also the growing remittances which act as a cushion to the increasing oil prices.

As the job profile of Indian workers is changing and they switching over to white collar jobs, salaries are increasing and with it the need for new financial institutional cooperation. India is seeking cooperation with financial institutions in GCC states so as to cater to the growing financial needs of both the people. There is also a growing concern in India about the religions extremist groups in the GCC states targeting Indian workers due to developments in Iraq and elsewhere in the region as also due to India's close proximity to the United States and Israel.

The new NDA government in India led by the BJP is adopting a new approach to India's foreign policy with centrality being given to economic and technological development/ objectives.

One can notice continuity and change in the new government's foreign policy. There is no doubt the new NDA government will strengthen ties with Israel too.

Conclusion

India's old historical ties with GCC states coupled with the current presence of over six million Indian workers in the region, increasing imports of oil [over 70 percent] and gas, growing trade [20 percent of exports], aid and investments opportunities are vital interests of India. Due to growing imports of chemical fertilizers from GCC states, India's food security is now increasingly linked with the Gulf region.

From the strategic point of view, both India and GCC states share the need for political stability and the need to reduce the role of non-regional states whose policies are undermining peace, security and stability, leading to the periodic threats of military intervention. The common political and strategic concerns of India and GCC and the desire to work for the peace, security and stability in the Gulf region and South Asia and the emerging common threat perceptions will create opportunities in future. The past two decades have seen the reassertion of regional and local identities in the face of outside interference.

The GCC states are going through important changes and the process of reconciliation and understanding is maturing. The critical space is widening. It is in this context, that India and the GCC states can create opportunities for mutual benefit not only in the oil and gas sector, trade and commerce, sharing and development of human resources, but also for mutual security and joint preparation to meet emerging domestic and regional challenges.

Many argue that India's ardour for the Arab cause has waned and become muted. Most Arab states including the GCC states despite having very close ties with the US and EU have been unable to restrain the US and others in blind support to Israel. Not only due to the collapse of USSR and the Kashmir issue but also due to a variety of other factors, India has been working hard to improve relations with the US.

India in co-operation with such like-minded states has been striving hard to remove the factors creating instability in the Gulf region. Both the GCC states and India face the menace of terrorism and religious extremism and the need to combat such forces. A modest beginning has been made for cooperation in the field of security with the GCC states which has a rich potential field ahead.

So far, Indian diplomacy has been fairly successful in containing the negative impact flowing from domestic issues on India's relations with the GCC states. The policy of the Modi government has been quite balanced towards the region taking into account the manifold interests and geo-strategic considerations.

What is to be noted is that things are rapidly changing in the region and India must always be careful in managing the relationship in the region that are of utmost importance to India's national interests.

References

Agwani, M.S. (2009), "Global War on Terrorism", *Journal of Strategic Studies*, Vol. 5, No. 17, winter, pp. 17-36.

Chatterjee, Kingshuk (2009), "India's Relationships with the Gulf Region: Prospects and Possibilities in the 21st Century", in Ghosh, Anjali et al. (ed.), 'India's Foreign Policy', New Delhi: Pearson, pp. 357-378.

Dahiya, Rumel (ed.) (2014), "Developments in the Gulf Region: Prospects and Challenges for India in the Next Two Decades", New Delhi: IDSA, Pentagon Press.

Embassy of India, (Riyadh), (2010), "Visit of Dr. Manmohan Singh to Saudi Arabia, February 27-March 1, 2010: A New Era of

Strategic Partnership", pp. 1-95.

Gopal, Krishan and Sarbjit Sharma (2007), "India and Israel: Towards Strategic Partnership", Delhi: Authors Press, pp. 99-212.

Gulf Research Centre (2009), "India's Growing Role in the Gulf: Implications for the Region and the United States", Dubai: Cambridge.

Gupta, Ranjit and Christian Koch, (ed.) (2013), "GCC-India Relations", Dubai: Gulf Research Centre Foundation.

Gupta, Ranjit et al., (2014), "A New Gulf Security Architecture: Prospects and Challenges for an Asian Role", Berlin: Gerlach Press.

Gupta, Ranjit et al. (2013), "India and the Gulf: What Next?", Dubai: Gulf Research Centre.

Hiro, Dilip (2010), "After Empire: The Birth of a Multipolar World", New York: Nation Books, pp. 187-206.

Janardhan, N. (2007), "Gulf Security and India", *Gulf-Asia*, GRC, Gulf Research Centre, Dubai, No. 1 January, pp. 28-31.

Kapur, Harish (2009), "Foreign Policies of India's Prime Ministers", New Delhi: Lancers.

Kumaraswamy, P.R. (ed.) (2014), "Persian Gulf 2013: India's Relations with the Region", New Delhi: Sage Publications.

Menon, K.S.R. (2008) "India-Iran Relations: Tough Road Ahead", *Gulf-Asia*, No. 5, August, pp. 28-31.

Pant, G. (2007), "Energy Security in Asia: The Necessity of Interdependence", *Strategic Analysis*, Volume 31, No. 3, May, pp. 507-526.

Pant, Harsh V. (2009), "India and the Middle East: A Re-assessment of Priorities?" in Harsh V. Pant (ed.), 'Indian Foreign Policy in a Unipolar World', New Delhi: Routledge, pp. 251-276.

Pasha, A.K. (1993), "Tipu and the Ottoman Empire", in B. Sheik Ali, (ed.), 'Tipu Sultan: A Great Martyr', Bangalore University: Prasaranga, pp. 219-232.

—(1998), "India and the GCC", in A.K. Pasha and Riyaz Punjabi, (eds.) 'India and the Islamic World', New Delhi: Radiant Publishers, pp. 34-48.

—(2005), "India and the Gulf States: Challenges and Opportunities", Rajen Harshe and K.M. Seethi (eds.), 'Engaging with the World: Critical Reflections on India's Foreign Policy', New Delhi: Orient Longman, pp. 389-424.

——(2006), "Pax Americana in the Gulf Region: Implications for India's Quest for Energy Security", in S.N. Malakar (ed.), 'India's Energy Security and the Gulf', Delhi: Academic Excellence, pp. 116-122.

——(2006), "India's Policy towards the Arab World in the 21st Century" in V.D. Chopra (ed.), 'India's Foreign Policy in the 21st Century', Delhi: Kalpaz Publications, pp. 215-250.

——(2007), "Indian Perceptions on Persian Gulf", *World Focus*, Vol. XXVIII, Nos.11-12, November-December, pp. 446-457.

——(2008), "India's Policy towards the Persian Gulf" in G. Kishore Babu (ed.) 'India's Foreign Policy: Continuity and Change', Delhi: Academic Excellence, pp. 215-247.

——(2008), "Recent Developments in the Gulf Region: An Overview", *World Focus*, Vol. 39, No. 2, February, pp. 43-47.

——(2009), "India's Changing Threat Perceptions from West Asia", *Strategic Studies*, Bahrain, Vol. 5, No. 16, autumn, pp. 9-52.

——(2009), "India and Turmoil in West Asia: Challenges and Emerging Responses", *World Focus*, Vol. 30, Annual Number, November-December, pp. 484-490.

——(2009), "India and West Asia: Challenges and Opportunities", in Anjali Ghosh, et al. (ed.), 'India's Foreign Policy', Delhi: Pearson, pp. 301-356.

——(2007), "India and Gulf: An Overview", *World Focus*, Vol. XXVIII, No. 2, February, pp. 39-45.

——(2008), "Recent Developments in the Gulf Region: An Overview", *World Focus*, Vol. 39, No.2, February, pp. 43-47.

——(2009), "India's Changing Threat Perceptions from West Asia", *Strategic Studies*, Bahrain, Vol. 5, No.16, autumn, pp. 9-52.

——(2009), "India and Turmoil in West Asia: Challenges and Emerging Responses", *World Focus*, Vol. 30, Annual Number, November-December, pp. 484-490.

——(2010), "Struggle for Democracy and Civil Society in GCC States", in Sujata Ashwarya Cheema (ed.), 'West Asia: Civil Society, Democracy and State', New Delhi: New Century Publications, pp. 38-67.

——(2011), "Violence in West Asia: Implications for India's Federalism and Security" in G. Gopa Kumar (ed.), 'Foreign Policy, Federalism and International Treaties', New Delhi: New Century Publications, pp. 192-254.

——(2012), "India and the GCC States: Political, Economic and

Foreign Relations" in Kingshuk Chatterjee (ed.) 'India and the Middle East: Problems and Prospects', New Delhi: Knowledge World Publishers, pp. 25-65.

——(2013), "India's Changing Threat Perception from West Asia", in Mohd. Moazzam Ali Muztarib (ed.), 'Threat Perception in a Globalizing World with Special Reference to India', New Delhi: Gyan Publishing House, pp. 198-216.

——(2013), "Euro-Asian Maritime, Trade and Security Issues and the West Asian/Gulf Factor", in K.S. Pavithran (ed.), 'Foreign Policy and Maritime Security of India', New Delhi: New Century Publications, pp. 207-254.

——(2013), "Turmoil in West Asia and India's Quest for Energy Security," in Mohanan B. Pillai (ed.), 'India's National Security: Concerns and Strategies', New Delhi: New Century Publications, pp. 133-177.

——(2014), "India and Saudi Arabia: Retrospect and Prospects", in Mahmood, Fazal and Rafiullah Azmi (eds.), 'Foreign Policy of India and West Asia: Change and Continuity', New Delhi: New Century, pp. 187-216.

——(2014), "India and Gulf Cooperation Council [GCC] States", in Shaji Varkey (ed.), 'Globalization, State and Governance', New Delhi, New Century Publications, pp. 23-49.

——(2014), "India and the Gulf Region: Maritime History, Trade, Security and Political Reforms", Delhi: Wisdom Publications.

——(2014), "India and the GCC States: Historical, Geopolitical and Strategic Perspectives", Delhi: Wisdom Publications.

——(2014), "India's Political and Foreign Relations with the Gulf Region", Delhi: Wisdom Publications.

Pardesi, Manjeet S. and Sumit Ganguly (2009), "India and Energy Security: A Foreign Policy Priority", in Harsh V. Pant (ed.), 'Indian Foreign Policy in a Unipolar World', New Delhi: Routledge, pp. 99-127.

Pradhan, Samir R. (2010), "India and the GCC: An Economic and Political Perspective", *Strategic Analysis*, Volume 34, No.1, January, pp. 93-103.

Pradhan, Samir Ranjan (2008), "Indo-Gulf Relations: Mapping Strategic Dimensions", *Gulf-Asia*, No. 5, August, pp. 14-21.

Riaz, Harun (2006), "India-Saudi Arabia in Focus", January, pp. 1-62.

Sikri, Rajiv (2009), "Challenge and Strategy: Rethinking India's Foreign Policy", New Delhi: Sage Publications.

Singh, B.K. (2010), "India's Energy Security: The Changing Dynamics", New Delhi: Pentagon Press, pp. 15-50 and 101-133.

Strategic Digest (2008), "India-Saudi Arabia", Volume 38, No. 5, May, pp. 567-573.

5

India's Policy in Latin America

Binay Prasad

In the present time, when India's foreign policy approach is being reassessed and strategies being redesigned, probably India' entry in 'unconventional' regions of the world has gathered much attention. From a rational point of view, while every region holds and deserves equal importance, it is unfortunate and fortunate as well; India has over the years prioritised the same based on its own perception.

The region which has received a significant attention in recent times is Latin America and Caribbean (LAC), as India seems to take trade opportunities in consideration. While India is seriously taking other unexplored regions of the world on its diplomatic umbrella, Latin America is a region that comes with the least "political baggage". It implies while India establishes diplomatic links with LAC, it does not have to be concerned with the past of political relations or in present times, the political implications of the decisions it would take in the process (Bhojwani, 2014: 4). In simple terms, India would by virtue only be missing available opportunities if it commits mistakes but would be exempted of serious injury like in case of dealing with volatile regions of the world.

Historical Antecedents

The projection of India's entry in LAC to be 'new' is rather ambiguous but true as India's intermingling with countries of LAC has been more vigorous and fast paced in recent years than in several past decades. This is not to say that these two regions did not have a history of any connection at the diplomatic or non-diplomatic level. Though contestable, but not totally refutable; literatures and litterateurs from both sides derive civilisational linkages and is evident from the hard to believe and tough to counter, similar societal practices and social belief systems that exists; resemble linkages between the two (Narayanan, 1988: 5-6; Chaudhary, 1992: 116-118). All aside, either during the colonial period or even in post-Independence era, low profile political contacts did exist. The common links of Portuguese rule in Brazil in LAC and Goa in India are well-founded.

On the cultural side, Indian literature and philosophy appealed Latin Americans. This can be invariably ascertained from the reports sent by the Press Attaché of Indian missions. Gandhi's and Nehru's philosophy received a place in the news articles that appeared in Latin American presses. This, however, is not to be said that Indian culture and political thinking took all of Latin Americans aboard. Conversely, those who were moved by Indian philosophy were nothing but a minute section of elites who had developed an interest in the culture and the literature of the East. Interestingly, Rabindranath Tagore stayed in Argentina for a significant time period and served as a state guest of Peru in 1924, and several other Latin American countries.

Even during 18th century; British India by default had diplomatic linkages with the islands of the Caribbean. During the 18th century, a massive number of indentured labourers were taken to Caribbean countries to work in the sugar plantations and to oversee this, Indian legations were set up in those regions by the British government. Besides Caribbean countries, even in Latin American Countries, India had trade missions like the one in Argentina, which was set up way back in 1943. After India's Independence, the formal separation of India British Foreign Office and Ministry of External Affairs took place and hence foreign policy took a separate course.

India's Independence and LAC

Foreign relations between two entities are largely driven

by a 'policy' classified as under 'foreign policy' in the present international relations. As far as India's Latin American policy is concerned, India's Independence from the British rule marked a turning point. Though, India even before it had established diplomatic relations with LAC, it had to face the problems of Indians residing and working there. With the partition of India in 1947, most Indians in LAC were clueless like MEA was, pertaining to the issue of citizenship and concern over countering the anti-India reporting that swept the Latin American presses, and those of Argentina in particular. In other words, Indian missions had a major task i.e. to defend India's image in a region, where its image was yet to be built in political and diplomatic sense.

Subsequently, India's diplomatic relations with LAC were established, prioritising major countries in the region over smaller ones. In other words, India's diplomatic presence was not mere presence, but also an attempt to defend India's position on the question of Kashmir, Hyderabad and Goa. These political questions were significant in reference to India's sovereignty and integrity. It was equally important for existence of India as a political entity. This is not to say that the countries in Latin American region had a stake in all those political questions.

In reality, barring the question of Goa and other Portuguese colonies in which Brazil was directly involved being a mediator in the issue, the situation was different in other cases. In other cases, while no major Latin American country had a stake, but they became indirectly involved, as several countries of LAC served their term as non-permanent members of the UN Security Council. That too, at a time, when such important political questions pertaining to India's claim were being discussed there. Indian governments' concern was to develop a pro-India posture making available substantial arguments and facts to the foreign offices of the respective Latin American countries.

Indian foreign policy faced serious challenges in developing a consensus in favour of India on the question of Kashmir and Hyderabad. Similarly, India also tried its best in gaining moral sympathy from Latin American countries in the wake of the Chinese aggression in 1962 as well as East Bengal operation in 1971. As an exception, Goa issue was the only issue that brought a Latin American country directly involved in the issue of India's dispute with Portugal. On the issue of Goa, as diplomatic relations between India and Portugal were snapped in 1957; Brazil at the request of Portugal, took up the charge as a mediator between India and Portugal. The period denotes a diplomatically tense relation between India and Brazil.

It is revealed from the reports sent by Indian embassy at Rio de Janeiro to MEA that in the case of Goa, Brazilian journalist and academicians at the request of Indian diplomats, contributed to news stories and features putting India's claim of Goa. It appears from this, what appeared in Brazilian press on its own, favouring India's position was nothing but few. In other cases as well, India's presence was merely on the basis of the articles that appeared on India in the Latin American presses by the way of Western news agencies. The complexity of Goa case also revealed that the actual situation of the Portuguese ruled Goa was not even known to the Brazilian journalists. In fact, in 1954, while at the interaction between Indian and Brazilian journalists, the latter on hearing about Goa from the Indian journalists, expressed surprise at the version which was rather a distorted one that was available to them in Brazil.

India's Policy and its Perception

Of late, India neither had a consistent Latin American policy nor was much familiar with the LAC region. As we move ahead to design a Latin American policy, we must look at the past failures, that were committed by India in the region and revisit the old perceptions and lenses with which India saw the issues of Latin America.

First and foremost, India being a widely known country in

Latin America and Caribbean is partially true, as it remained familiar to political elites alone. Secondly, repeated usage and association of non-alignment ideology with countries of Latin America, was nothing more than a myth. Thirdly, in past several decades, even the reports received from Indian embassies in Latin America explicitly denote that not only in action but also in the wording pattern, the Latin American policy remained more a suggestive one than a deliberative one.

A most discussed issue that shaped the perception of Indian diplomacy during the Cold War era; neutralism and Third Worldist thinking did not apply to Latin America as assumed (Roy, 2010: 392, 393). Contrary to the belief, Latin American nations are a third world country unlike Third World, as they remained purely European in outlook all through 50s and 60s and decades later (Nafey, 1988: 87). Much a fuss about enthusiasm of Latin American nations towards Non-Alignment Movement is also not true, as their official statements suggest that they considered this policy to be "foreign" to Latin America. In the initial phase, Latin American nations did not show much interest and Cuba remained the sole participant as a 'full member' to the NAM conference. Most countries in the continent considered joining NAM as inviting communist infiltration.

In the backdrop, it requires a mention; despite most countries having a neutral policy and association with the third world countries on the economic issues, did not ever reflect, that they were associated with the projected ideology of India. This in particular, is applicable in cases when Latin American countries saw the economic policies of United States and European nations hampering the economic interests of Latin American countries, when they went along with Third world bloc. Even on the issue of decolonisation, they differed with India's position.

To add further, a good example of disenchantment with neutralist and Third Worldist foreign policy is evident from a specific case of Brazil. The rise and the subsequent fall of Janio

Quadros, who was the President of Brazil resembles a perfect example. Quadros' rise in the 1960 Brazil national election owing to his commitment to take out Brazil from the 'clutches' of US imperialism was evident, but the accusation against him of allowing communist penetration in the political system of Brazil, not only compelled him to resign, but expelling his successor Goulart as well, under a military coup in 1964.

Adding further, a much established myth around India's popularity over NAM fell apart, going through a public opinion survey conducted by *Jornal do Brasil*, a prominent Brazilian newspaper. The survey was conducted after Indira Gandhi's visit to Brazil and other Latin American countries in 1968. The survey revealed that even after Indira Gandhi's visit, a substantial part of Brazilian population did not seem familiar of India's 'neutralist' foreign policy.

These empirical evidences prove that India's relation with Latin America existed on ambiguous familiarity of each other's problems and policies (Vargas, 2014; Bhojwani, 2014: 35). In most cases, there were little or no understanding of the latter's problems. However, optimistic part is that important political issues to the least received a space in the presses of this far off region. There are innumerable instances to cite which provide an insight into the way important political issues concerning India were being received by Latin American countries. One of such case is the 1962 Chinese aggression, in which barring Cuba and Brazil, most Latin American countries on record, criticised the Chinese action. Cuba and Brazil did not come out in open criticising the Chinese aggression.

Another important instance worth mentioning is the meeting of Latin American Parliament in 1971 at Caracas. Latin American Parliament (LAP) passed unanimously a resolution criticising the government and Army of Pakistan for the human rights abuses in East Bengal. It is interesting to note that India was the only country from outside the region to be invited to the meeting. At the political level, India found it comfortable to cope up with the situation in the above two mentioned cases.

Though not very far from these two events, were Khalistan movement, in which Ecuador was indirectly involved. The capital of Ecuador, Quito was the hot bed of pro-Khalistani activities and a Khalistan House was also established in Quito. The disturbing fact was that, there were reports related to Ecuador having recognised Khalistan, though it was 'promptly rejected' when the Indian government made representations to the Ecuadorian government. The significant point that requires mention here is that Ecuador had a substantial Sikh population adding different dimensions to the issue.

Learning from the Past Mistakes

Of late, India and Latin America have moved beyond these aberrations. Contrary to Latin American policy of Import Substitution Industrialisation (ISI) of 1950s and 1960s, end of the Cold War period marked the opening of Latin American countries, both in political and economic terms (Viswanathan, 2011: 7; Bhojwani, 2014: 36). As both the partners move up to design new strategies and new approaches to deal with each other, one must revisit the past to draw lessons for the future. It implies revisiting prejudiced perceptions. Hence, for instance, in the present time, India must look at the arguments against it which solidifies India's views about the Latin America region and its people through Brazilian lens.

The argument does have strength as most of the visible things like trade and South-South diplomacy are strictly limited to Brazil alone. In the backdrop of it, India must remember that Brazil is not Latin America. Additionally, India must not interpret Brazil as the gateway to LAC. It is in context of the rival and conflicting interests of several small and large nations of South America and Latin America, who might not relate themselves with the 'rising' Brazil. Similarly, Brazil's rise as a leader in South America or Latin America is inherently constrained by the things that keep Brazil and other countries in Latin American regions apart. Hence, India's success would be largely dependent on the perception which sees each nation of the continent as a separate political and cultural entity.

As far as India's Latin American Policy is concerned; the political reports, annual reports be it of 1950s or of 1970s kept suggesting about a prospective Latin American Policy. Nothing much materialised in the period. For example, the visit of the first Parliamentary delegation as well as Press delegation from Brazil to India took as late as 1964. A decade before i.e. in 1954, three Indian journalists had gone to Brazil to participate in the World Congress of Press Entities. The Indian diplomatic mission which was at Rio de Janeiro wished to seek this opportunity to hold an interaction with Brazilian journalists, to answer the question on the complexity of Goa issue. To the surprise, Indian diplomatic officials got to know from the Indian journalists that they were not even briefed by the Government of India, what was expected out of this visit. The instance referred here is to highlight the fallacies on the part of MEA.

The problems of past also reflect India's complacency of Latin America's support on the premise of Third Worldism, which was unfounded. In the backdrop, current policy of India must be structured to make India not only visible in Latin America but also India's policy more viable in face of the real and perceived challenges it faces or would face in the near future if not later. It is a reality, that contemporary India-Latin America links are trade driven, primarily, due to relations of both being itself an outcome of globalisation and liberalisation post-1990s.

The excuse of distance should be subsided, as similar distances and duration also measure up to United States and several other countries. The lack of political will and putting at stake the required resources has in reality, overemphasised the distance factor (Roy, 2010: 393). There are no direct flights yet to any of the 34 Latin American countries. It is, however, commendable that regular Air India flights to major Latin American capitals have become a reality. Those who travel in these are mostly business travellers, a phenomenon that puts trade upfront. These elements often project trade to be the sole lynchpin of India-Latin America links, downplaying other factors. In reality, India and Latin America have more to offer each other in real terms.

Making India Visible

The issue that posed a big challenge to the Indian diplomacy is quite evident now. Over the years, India-Latin America relations have proved India's diplomatic presence in LAC to be disparate. Interestingly, after Independence, only three countries of LAC had diplomatic exchanges with India. The average rate at which India developed diplomatic relations with the countries of Latin America stands at merely three in every ten years.

India still does not have a diplomatic representation to the level of Embassy in all Latin American countries. The Indian embassies in major Latin American countries serve as a non-resident mission of small neighbouring nations. The list also consists of those countries which have diplomatic representation at the level of embassy in India, but India does not have a resident mission in those countries. The scale of diplomatic expansion needs to be enhanced in Indian Foreign Service in general and with a focus on LAC in particular.

Indian Diaspora

It is an uncontestable fact that role of a country's diaspora remains significant in making a nation's presence felt. It is in this context that the role of Indian Diaspora in LAC cannot be undermined as far as the visibility of India in Latin American region is concerned. The Indian Diaspora in Caribbean region, only in recent decades has witnessed a pro-active policy to develop linkages between India and the Caribbean region (Gangopadhyay, 2005). In such a process, India seems to forget that, Caribbean alone is not the place of Indian origin people. Indians belonging to various religious and cultural communities reside across Latin American region. A serious initiative is awaited to accomplish establishing linkages with those small groups.

Academic Linkages

A most significant and unattended issue is that of academics (Vargas, 2014: 189-191). A limited number of universities in India, to be precise only two namely Jawaharlal Nehru University and Goa University at present conduct advanced teaching and research in the field of the Latin American Studies. Some other institutions have started the Latin American Studies Programmes on a modest scale.

Academic linkages do exist though they remain solely under the ambit of respective universities without a much needed institutional support from the Indian government. On the governmental level, a programme called Indian Technical and Economic Cooperation (ITEC) offers technical training to students in the Latin American region in the field of engineering and technology. Similarly, by default, Brazil's *Ciencia Sem Fronteiras* (Science without Borders) has established academic and research links with institutions involved in research and teaching in the field of sciences.

Hence, the stream of social sciences remains on the wayside. Even languages, namely Spanish and Portuguese, remains outside the ambit of the initiatives of the government. The point of language being a barrier between India and Latin America does not seem true, as the interest to learn Spanish and Portuguese language in India is no less. The cultural institutes of Spanish and Portuguese government, i.e. *Instituto Cervantes* and *Instituto Camoes*, has been over the years offering language training, and the interest in India towards such programmes is rather huge. Contrary to it, no initiatives at the level of Indian government to invite Spanish and Portuguese speakers for Latin American region to offer language courses have formalised yet. In fact, inviting native speakers to offer language courses at Indian universities and schools would not only be an economical way of imparting foreign language education in India but also an effective one.

Looking at the Future

In making a distinct image of its own, India projects and feels proud of itself being a democracy as opposed to the case of China. However, the utility of having a democratic country as a partner is of lesser importance to LAC, if India is not in a position to offer tangible benefits to Latin American democracies which are still in their formative phase of democratic consolidation. This is also a factor that constrains India's ability to do what it wishes and at the pace that is required, in comparison to China, which retains its vigorous nature. It implies that, if trade is being run purely in economic terms, then India has nothing to gain being a democracy which China is not. Though a point worth mentioning here is that probably India's position as a democratic nation and its pattern of diplomacy has provided a soft image to it, in the sense, that India's presence in Latin America is not seen as a threat but China's presence is. When it comes to offering, India can do the least to share its democratic experience of over six decades with the countries of Latin America. India can intermingle at the bilateral level with the institutions of LAC helping strengthen their democratic institutions. This can range from assistance on electoral process to the highly specialised assistance on legislative, executive and judiciary level.

Recent decades have witnessed regional integration process to be a significant contributor in democratisation and democratic consolidation process. India has not actually involved itself in various regional organisations of Latin American region, which are delved into strengthening democratic institutions by way of trade organisations and agreements which involve, what has come to be known as the 'democracy clause'. India limiting itself to major entities like

Mercosur (Market for the Southern Cone) would eventually, be left out of the available opportunities in other smaller but significant regional blocs. India would be most importantly at the receiving end from such initiatives (Heine, 27: 2011). Even agreements between India and other regional grouping in LAC are yet to see a pro-active 'follow-up'.

India's Perception of its Soft Power in LAC

An established belief in Indian perception is of India having taken Latin America aboard through its soft power. The primary reasons for such beliefs are the articles that fill the spaces of websites magazines of how popular India is in this far-off land. In reality, most of these things grew on its own, having not anything on the part of Indian diplomatic circles. While there is no doubt of Indian culture to be appealing to Latin Americans, but projection of the same of being universal is unfounded. Over the years, Latin Americans have set up several fan associations, hence a Bollywood of their own.

As Indian initiative is to be measured, there can nothing be more surprising than the fact that, there are only a limited number of Indian cultural centres in LAC, out which three are in Caribbean region which itself needs to be increased. This contrasts with rather massive presence of Confucius Institutes of China in LAC. In principle, the ICCR cultural centres till date are purely cultural institutes, as opposed to Confucius Institutes which do have inherent political objectives. Some other initiatives are limited to Cultural Attaché of the Indian missions and the Chairs set up by ICCR (Indian Council of Cultural Relations) either with or without collaboration of the Indian MEA. Adding to it, tourism is one such an area, which can go a long way in projecting one's image abroad. In a recent initiative that provides advance registration for on-arrival visa to foreign tourists—it is in fact worth a praise that the list has been significantly extended. The initial programme included only two countries, namely Mexico and Brazil from LAC.

As far as projection of soft power is concerned, Bollywood seems to have taken a front stage, putting literary circles on the backstage. Another point that requires attention is that, even now when it comes to exhibiting the literary heritage of India, the country seems to live on its past legacy. This is in reference to reliance on Indian epics and Spanish translations of major works of Tagore to be the sole thing to project abroad. Even when Bollywood has hegemonised the stage, India seems less eager to monetise that. This implies, as most of the serious works are being done from the side of Latin Americans, Indian side has not embarked upon deriving financial benefit out of that.

Re-assessment of the Terms of Trade

On trade matters as well, India has not yet put its state-owned secondary and tertiary level companies in the Latin American region, which would make it move ahead, making trade linkages more viable. The logic to induct secondary and tertiary level sectors in Latin America is largely based on the fact that Latin American region needs more sectors in this field. Hence, India and Latin America both exchanging raw materials would not continue for long as a viable option (Vargas, 2014: 191). The viability is constrained in face of the increased competition from heavy machinery units being set up in LAC by developed countries of the world. In a similar way, India's growing pharmaceutical sector which has already made a place in the markets of the developed regions of world with low cost generic drugs is yet to receive a significant place in its Latin American journey.

In fact, Latin American region would prove to be a good market for the low cost medicines manufactured by Indian companies. On the contrary, statistics suggest that the pharmaceutical sector has shown a declining trend. There has been much discussion in the business circles on the 'financing' part of such business initiatives. As opposed to Chinese financial institutions, Indian financial institutions have expressed their inability to offer line of credit at cheaper rates

(Bhojwani, 2014: 39). This needs to be worked out by enhancing the quality of investments (Vargas, 2014: 191-192). To move further, Indian and Latin American financial sectors can also start collaboration on micro credit financing, which has taken a leap forward in LAC.

China Factor

Either in terms of referring India in Latin America or otherwise, China holds a significant place. Scholars have pointed the 'downfall' of United States in LAC to be the primary reason; China and India have made a place in the continent. In such a situation, if on every parameter, China and India are being compared and scaled, Latin America is no exception to such a measurement. Even by a rough estimate, India's trade volume with Latin America is being challenged by a more serious partner of Latin America i.e. China. In face of it, India needs to consider a strategy either to compete or to adopt a complementary policy. Of late, it is an accepted argument that India either in terms of capability or even by a similar intention do not wish to compete with China (Roy, 2010: 388). In such a case, India needs to adopt a viable trade policy. Some complementary initiatives are likely to materialise with joint bidding process by China and India for oil explorations in Latin America.

As discussed earlier, India which is largely a supplier and buyer of raw materials of Latin American countries, needs to move ahead of this primitive stage of product exchange. China has already taken extensive manufacturing work in Latin American countries or doing the same in its own territory by importing the raw materials from LAC and is fairly ahead of India. The lack on the part of willingness of Indian government is clearly visible, as far as the present case is concerned. As opposed to China, whose state-owned enterprises have penetrated Latin America, the government of Indian side have pushed largely the private sector to start their operations in Latin America and the Caribbean.

The situation discussed here poses a practical problem, i.e. in fulfilling the strategic objectives of the government in absence of state-led enterprises in the region. Private enterprises on the other hand are profit driven, staying aloof from what a government's possible strategy may be. The disinterest is on the premise that such grand initiatives would overstretch India's public sector. Additionally, promotion of India's private sector to start operations in foreign countries has been in consonance of India's business culture till date. Hence in this case, China and it state-owned sectors are well ahead of India. Even otherwise, China is much ahead of other Asian investors like Japan and South Korea in Latin America.

What Latin America Can Offer?

As emphasised earlier, India's policy in Latin America is severely constrained by inherent limitations encompassing India's capability and willingness to take up serious tasks in LAC. However, despite such limitations, India would be a significant beneficiary of what Latin American countries has to offer. Tangible and intangible benefits both await India to exploit. Latin America as a big market, is a known fact, but there is more for India. Latin American countries and Brazil in particular have a long experience in climate change negotiations with the developed countries on bilateral terms and with international as well as regional organisations on multilateral terms. India which itself is involved in environmental negotiations at the bilateral as well as at multilateral level can learn a lot from the tactics deployed by Latin American countries for the same.

In the last one decade, several Latin American countries have successfully implemented poverty alleviation programmes like *Fome zero* and *Bolsa Familia* in Brazil to *Oportunidades* (now known as *Prospera*) in Mexico. Success stories of such programmes can be helpful to India, as India wishes to secure developmental goals in definite period of time. Latin America comes in a big way to help India secure its energy needs as most Latin American countries have developed high-level expertise in manufacture of bio-diesel and other agro-based sources of energy (Viswanathan, 2011: 14). In terms of research, Brazil and Argentina have in recent years gone far ahead in innovation of new technologies in the field of agriculture (Viswanathan, 2011: 15).

In the current scenario, threats from terrorist attacks and other similar attacks from rebel groups have mounted exponentially. India and Latin America both suffer from similar threats and hence scope for cooperation is large. India can collaborate with security agencies and machineries of the Colombian government who have expertise in handling terror related operations as well as trafficking activities (Katju, 2011: 5-6).

In the current scenario, India sees itself as emerging power and wishes a significant place at the international level. In the backdrop, India must pay attention to not only major South American countries for political support but most significantly towards small Caribbean nations each of which have a vote at the United Nations. India and Latin America can collaborate for institutional strengthening which is the need of the hour (Vargas, 2014: 192).

Conclusion

As Latin America and India have been rightly called "partners in progress", much is need to progress at the level of relations between the two partners. Serious level diplomatic decisions need to be taken to increase involvement at the political, economic and cultural front at the same time. India must make full utilisation of the fact that India-Latin America relations does not come with any political baggage embedded in it. Additionally, India must not only move to advanced phase in trade relations but also move beyond trade. India has a lot to learn from Latin America. Latin America brings both tangible and intangible benefits for India, which sees itself to be a significant player in the global arena. In serious terms, a serious Latin American policy needs to be devised for the 21st century.

References

Bhojwani, Deepak (2014), "India and Latin America: Looking Ahead", *India Quarterly*, 70(1), 33-46.

Chaudhary, N.P. (1990), "India's Latin America Relations", New Delhi: South Asian Publishers.

Gangopadhya, Aparajita (2005), "India's Policy towards its Diaspora: Continuity and Change", *India Quarterly*, 61(93), 93-122.

Heine, Jorge (2011), "Much to Gain by Working Together in the Emerging International Order" *Indian Foreign Affairs Journal*, 6(1), 19-27.

Jadeja, Daulatsinghji P. (ed.) (1988), "India and Latin America: Partners in Progress", New Delhi: Trans Asia Publications.

Katju, Vivek (2011), "Growing Awareness between India and Latin America", *Indian Foreign Affairs Journal*, 6(1), 3-6.

Roy, Ash Narain Roy (2010), "Latin America in India's Foreign Policy", *International Studies*, 47(2-4), 387-440.

Vargas, Soraya Caro (2014), "India-Latin America: An Alliance for the Future", New Delhi: Vitasta.

Viswanathan, R. (2011), "The New Latin America and the Next Steps for India", *Indian Foreign Affairs Journal*, 6(1), 7-18.

- A substantial number of arguments and inputs in the paper have been derived from the personal reading of declassified materials of MEA. Hence, such arguments/inputs have not been cited or mentioned in the reference list.

6

India and European Union in the 21st Century

Mathew Sinu Simon

India and European Union have been 'sharing common perspectives on multiculturalism, diversity and plural societies'. Both India and EU also 'share a commitment to democratic principles and judicial values, the safeguarding of human rights, human development and a vibrant media'. This commonality of perspectives and shared interests has often led to dubbing of India and EU as 'natural partners'. Former Prime Minister Dr. Manmohan Singh remarked that the economies of India and EU are complementary to each other. [1]

India is a sovereign state that finds difficult to understand the foreign policy orientations of the EU. EU is a complex entity combining inter-governmentalism and supranationalism [2] that at times does not have a coherent strategy on foreign policy. The member states of EU often compete with each other or major European states have a greater say leading to a divided house. There have been efforts, however, through founding treaties and the subsequent ones like the Lisbon Treaty to streamline the processes of integration towards the idea of 'one voice, one Europe'. [3]

In the twenty-first century, the foreign policy strategies of India and EU have evolved considerably. Economy is the core of this strategy. With the institutionalization of summits and formalization of partnership in 2000, India and EU have engaged in diverse fields like technology transfer, climate change and civil society exchanges. Since 2000, in the Summits, 'nothing of substance on strategic front has since been delivered other than notoriously lengthy agenda of activities and earnest statements never leading to action'. [4]

This paper attempts to briefly examine the concept of foreign policy strategy in the 21st century. It then analyses the strategic nature and foreign policy orientations of India-EU relationship as enunciated in 2004. It explores the reasons thereof for the missed opportunities and lapses between India and EU in their foreign policy strategies. There is a brief review of the security aspects of strategic cooperation in counter-terrorism, cyber security and anti-sea piracy operations. The future areas of cooperation which include among others, the civilian nuclear energy, sustainable development and trade and investment agreement are discussed. It is argued that such cooperation provides ground for strengthening strategies between India and EU in the 21st century.

Defining Foreign Policy Strategies

The word strategy derives from the Greek word 'strategus'. [5] It means generalship and is put to wider use in game theory. A strategy is a plan for dealing with every possible move by the other player(s) at every stage in the game. The best possible strategy is sought to achieve a specific purpose. It is a plan designed to achieve a particular long-term aim. There are different strategies used in planning and directing a military activity in a war. It is done so with the intention of gaining a long-term military advantage.

A foreign policy [6] may be defined as the policy formulated and pursued by a political system in order to promote the collective interest of that system in relation to other political systems. The political system employs various means and measures to achieve foreign policy objectives. It was A.P. Rana who used the term foreign policy strategy. [7]

Taylor once remarked that in international relations, "foreign policy of a sort will go on so long as there are sovereign states". [8] Broadly, foreign policy includes objectives, plans and actions taken by a state relative to its external relationships. In a narrow sense, it refers to actions (including words) of government officials to influence human behaviour beyond the jurisdiction of their own state. Padelford and Lincoln maintained that "foreign policy is the key element in the process by which a state translates its broadly conceived goals and interests into concrete courses of actions to attain those objectives and preserve its interests". [9]

Charles Burton Marshall argues that in foreign policy, "utterances is sometimes a form of action and pronouncements are deeds when they convey meaning about things intended to be done rather than merely expressing abstractions and moralization". [10] Mahendra Kumar defines foreign policy "as a thought out course of action for achieving objectives in foreign relations as dictated by the ideology of national interests". [11]

According to H.J. Morgenthau's realist theory, foreign policy has two basic principles. Firstly, it is used as a lever to secure national interest, (whatever interests might be) and secondly, foreign policy has to be framed in a fashion that commitments are equal to the capacity for fulfilling them. [12] Lerche and Said posited three elements of foreign policy to include: (i) formulation of the objective in the most precise terms possible; (ii) the nature of action undertaken, stated with sufficient clarity to guide and direct the state's other officials; and (iii) the forms and perhaps the amount of national power involved. [13]

A foreign policy strategy is the strategy of a government in dealing with other nations. The policy of the government on foreign affairs consists of strategies determined to safeguard its national interests. For example, the Reagan Doctrine in the United States foreign policy during the eighties prescribed a course of action that supported anti-communist revolutions. India adopted a policy of non-alignment during the Cold War era to avoid being a part of the two prominent military blocs. Strategies at the foreign policy level constantly evolve and are determined by varied set of factors like domestic public opinion, economy and international scenarios.

In the 21st century, with the attacks on twin towers in US, war in Iraq, Iranian nuclear sanctions, the Arab Spring, rise of

Islamic State, Eurozone and Ukraine crisis, strategizing foreign policy has become a complex activity. The processes of foreign policy decision-making in a country are also increasingly influenced by non-state actors, regional groupings, coalitions and alliances. National interests of the governments still anchors and prioritize the goals of foreign policy. In a complex and interdependent globalizing world, through technology, market and people, foreign policy strategies have faced challenges and missed opportunities.

European Union Foreign Policy Strategies

There are definitional problems in evaluating European Union foreign policy strategies. As foreign policy is about the capability and capacity of a state to influence global politics, EU does not easily fit into this category. As said by a scholar studying EU, "EU is an intergovernmental and supranational and almost state like. The major difference is that it is almost state like but not a state and so it is not a unified single actor like a state". [14]

The European Community grew amidst German reunification and collapse of Soviet Union that bought an end to the Cold War. The Maastricht Treaty of 1992 provided EU a new institutional capability. The Common Foreign and Security Policy (CFSP) gave visibility that was lacked earlier. The Community acquired "civilian" [15] forms of power in an attempt to be a separate military identity to NATO. The adoption of Petersberg tasks (1992) were put to test with the onset of Balkan crisis. However, the four wars in the Balkans—Slovenia (19991), Croatia (1992-93), Bosnia (1992-95) and Kosovo highlighted the political and institutional incapacity of the EU to respond to the crisis.

In midst of these failures, the EU launched its first civilian mission under the ESDP in Bosnia and Herzegovina and dispatched a European Union Police Mission (EUPM) on January 1, 2003. Operation Concordia was launched on March 31, 2003 in the former Yugoslav Republic of Macedonia. Concordia was a success of Berlin Plus arrangements and provided grounds for cooperation between EU and NATO. The first military operation of EU, independent of NATO was Operation Artemis in the Democratic Republic of Congo on June 12, 2003. The mandate was to stabilize the security conditions until a reinforced UN mission in Congo (MONUC) was deployed. It earned praise from then UN Secretary General Kofi Annan for positive and quick response of EU in providing assistance to UN.

From the above cases, it shows that the external actions of EU as a civilian power have acquired a distinct military capability. However, the ability of EU to respond collectively to crisis came into question with the events of 9/11 and the war in Iraq. The causes were divisions among the member states and clash of interests with the US. So, without a strategy, "belated reactions, decision-making paralysis and coalitions of the willing outside the EU framework were the likely outcome". [16]

The European Council in its meeting in Brussels adopted the European Security Strategy (ESS) in December 2003. The document was entitled "A Secure Europe in a Better World: The European Security Strategy". [17] The strategic objectives as enunciated were: (a) to address the threats as a global actor, and (b) to build security in the neighbourhood pertaining to: (i) the Balkans, (ii) the neighbours in the east, (iii) the Southern Caucasus and (iv) the Euro-Mediterranean partnership.

The Council also defined four priority areas of action: (a) "effective multilateralism" with the UN at its core, (b) the fight against terrorism, (c) strategy towards the region of the Middle East, and (d) policy towards Bosnia-Herzegovina. The adoption of the ESS is a landmark and turning point to make EU as a full-fledged global actor. The Treaty of Lisbon (2009) created a High Representative of the Union for Foreign Affairs and Security Policy, de facto merging the post of High Representative for the Common Foreign and Security Policy and the European Commissioner for External Relations and European Neighbourhood Policy.

The Security Strategy urged that the EU "should look to

develop strategic partnerships" with Japan, China, Canada and India as well as with those who share our goals and values and are prepared to act in their support". [18] It made sense for EU to cooperate more closely with each of six countries as "key international players" in addressing the challenges and objectives identified in the strategy. Partnership with each of them will, therefore, develop in "different ways". [19]

India-EU Strategic Partnership

Recently, the term 'strategic partnership' has gained currency. In newspapers, it is common to read the headlines stating that India has forged 'strategic relations' or strategic partnerships with major global players. There is, however, no clear cut definition of what strategic partnership entails. Dr. Javier Solana, the High Representative for Common and Foreign Security, once remarked in an interview to a Chinese news agency that there is "no definition" of a strategic partnership in 2004. [20] The Indian Minister for Commerce and Industry, Kamal Nath, commented on strategic partnership as being "a convergence of beliefs and a shared vision of the future of the world". [21]

The first Indian diplomatic mission was established in Brussels in 1962. A joint political framework (1993) and cooperation agreement (1994) provided a legal and political basis of relationship between India and the European Union (EU). In 2000, India-EU summit and official level talks were initiated. The progress was made in 2004 by establishing a 'strategic' partnership between both the parties.

The 2004 strategic partnership [22] was an attempt to streamline and increase its effectiveness by broadly identifying five areas for interaction:

- Co-operation at international fora on multilateralism, human trafficking and migration, conflict prevention and post-conflict reconstruction, non-proliferation of weapons of mass destruction, promotion of democracy and protection of human rights.

- Economic co-operation–joint dialogues at sector level on regulatory and industrial policies.
- Development cooperation.
- Intellectual, scientific and cultural cooperation.
- Co-operation on the improvement of the institutional collaboration between India and the EU.

A joint action plan (2005) was formulated and several joint working groups on trade, investment, science and technology etc., were constituted to broaden the strategic nature of the relationship.

Traditionally, India had strong long standing relations with many individual European states which are now a part of the EU. These relations have continued uninterrupted. Whether the treaties between India and individual European states have a bearing on EU as a whole, is a moot point. But there exists an understanding, even agreements between EU as a whole in the domain of science and technology (2007), nuclear fusion energy research (2009), civil aviation (2008), and customs (2004).

However, the growing body of literature about ties between India and the European Union shows that there is no deepening or policy substance in diplomatic and especially security relations. Scholars working on Indo-EU relations have eluded strategic partnership to that of "loveless arranged marriage", [23] "charade", [24] a "directionless courtship" [25] and "strategically irrelevant". [26] Rajendra K. Jain, shares another view, suggesting that "India has [...] difficulty perceiving the European Union as a major actor on the international scene, as much regarding economic as political matters, and still, today, prefers good relations with the United States". [27]

This is neatly illustrated by Muenchow-Pohl who states, "India and the EU share common objectives, but these relate more to general principles for the global order than to details and deliverables. Geo-political distance and each side's preoccupation with its own neighbourhood contribute to a lack of genuine shared interests—apart from the fight against terrorism and piracy". [28] The bilateral ties between Delhi and Brussels may best be characterized as "lethargic" and this has "weakened the strategic value of this under-delivering partnership. There has been a clear gap in perceptions and priorities". [29]

Missed Opportunities in India-EU Strategic Partnership

It is imperative to understand that though the India-EU bilateral trade may have surpassed US$ 100 billion in 2011, yet there is a sharp imbalance between relative levels of trade between the two—where the EU accounts for roughly 21 percent of India's two way trade, India's share in the EU trade is less than one percent; where the EU is India's largest trading partner, India ranks 14th in the EU's list. Further, there may be an increase in FDI into India from the EU, but India still receives only 0.2 percent of the EU's FDI flows.

Unease in Doing Business in the European Market: Although India accepts EU as an economic superpower, most businessmen still think of doing business with individual member-states. They seem to be more interested in the British or German market rather than the European market. There is widespread belief that the EU is over-protectionist. [30] A large number of tariff and non-tariff barriers have become major deterrents in doing trade with the EU. In this context, the EU's health, quality standards and environmental and social laws are seen by many as a hindrance for the developing countries in business relations with the EU. India and the EU have been negotiating an FTA since 2007 but have not been able to finalize the accord due to differences over the EU's attempts to link trade with climate and other issues.

Misperceptions of India and EU towards Each Other: India does not take the collective identity of the EU at face value. Hence, it deals directly with the EU Commission on issues relating to trade and commerce. On the other hand, New Delhi has long maintained robust bilateral relations with the large EU member states such as the UK, France and Germany on political-security questions. Brussels simply lacks necessary instruments to ensure the kind of unity required in the political and security fields. Therefore, the EU is perceived as an incoherent and inconclusive political and security actor. This perception of disunity is largely a baggage from the past derived from the two Iraq wars of 1991 and 2003 and the disastrous Yugoslav conflict of the early 1990s.

Fundamental Differences between India and EU: The Indian view of EU foreign policy is also further conditioned by the fundamental differences between the two sides on many issues because of the facts that the two are at different levels of development, because they come from two vastly different regions and that they have different geopolitical priorities. Indian perceptions are conditioned by the fact that its historical experiences and realities are unique and that it inhabits in a very dangerous and unstable neighbourhood surrounded by failed or failing states and faces a variety of external threats and challenges. In spite of sharing values of democracy and human rights, there has been very little co-ordination between the two sides on attaining their goals in this regard. [31]

The EU provides very little value added to India's principal security challenges. In the immediate priority areas of strategic interest to India—our own neighbourhood, the Gulf region, the United States and China—the EU is almost irrelevant, and the story does not get better if one extends India's areas of security interest to Central and Southeast Asia. The EU also complains about the inadequate resources of the Ministry of External Affairs of the Government of India which is faced with the post-Lisbon European External Action Service as an extra peg to deal with. The recent sovereign debt crisis in the Eurozone has considerably dented the EU's image worldwide as also in the eyes of India. The solidarity and cohesion of the European Union faces perhaps the sternest test yet and it remains to be seen how the EU manages to overcome the crisis it faces at present.

Delays in Concluding BTIA talks: India and the EU have been negotiating a trade pact, also known as the Broad-based

Trade and Investment Agreement (BTIA), for about eight years. However, this could not be finalized because the EU has demanded a substantial tariff cut and the elimination of duties on European vehicles, auto components and wines and spirits. India, on the other hand, has sought more access to European markets, primarily the UK and Germany, for its professionals, under a relaxed Schengen visa regime. So far, there have been 15 rounds of talks on the BTIA, with the last round being held in 2013.

Italian Mariner's Issue: The recent case of the arrest of Italian marines for shooting Indian fishermen is a testimony of the growing strain in India-European Union relations. It also shows the influence of member states occupying the institutional policies at EU. This was reflected in the EU foreign policy chief, Italian by origin, condemning the action taken against Italian marines by Indian courts in a resolution passes in the European Parliament. According to the media reports, this is one of the reasons cited in not finalizing the dates for the India-EU summit for 2015. [32]

Areas for Co-operation

Cyber Security and Anti-sea Piracy Operations by India and EU: Cyber security has also been discussed between Indian foreign minister and the EU's High Representative. The EU and India meet annually in the context of the political dialogue on cyber security. EU also had information security dialogues with its strategic partners like Brazil, India, Russia, South Africa and South Korea. The joint naval anti-piracy operations involve India and the European Union (EU), who have joined hands for launching joint operations in the Indian Ocean. EU has deployed four warships and supporting military ships and aircrafts of EU member-countries and is engaged with the Indian Navy in developing synergy in the region.

Civil Society Exchanges and People-to-people Contacts: The framework of India-EU cooperation in the field of education and culture is provided by three Joint Declarations signed in recent years covering cooperation in the fields of education and training, multilingualism and culture. The first Senior Officials Meetings on Education and Multilingualism were held at Secretary Level in Brussels on May 25, 2011, followed by a second round in New Delhi on April 17, 2013. The Policy Dialogue on Culture was launched at the Secretary Level in New Delhi on April 18, 2013. The ERASMUS MUNDUS program has facilitated educational exchanges between India and Europe.

Energy Renewables: India and the EU set up an Energy Panel in 2005 for greater cooperation in the critical sector of energy and energy security. The last meeting of the Panel was held in New Delhi on November 18, 2011. Separate sub-groups have been constituted under the panel dealing with coal and clean coal conversion technologies, energy efficiency and renewable energy etc.

Bridging Digital Divide: After providing technical skills to 3,021 youths from backward districts of Tamil Nadu, Maharashtra and West Bengal, the New Emerging Technology (NET) Skills Project supported by the European Union (EU) and the Department of Science and Technology was replicated across India. A total of 1,800 youth from Tamil Nadu and 600 from West Bengal and Maharashtra benefited from the ₹ 8.25 crore project, which was funded by the EU. "The plan is to bridge the gap on the development front by focusing on bringing ashore NET skills for the benefit of the youth and adolescents of the backward regions of India", said Johann Hesse, counsellor and head of cooperation, delegation of EU to India. [33]

Conclusions

India and the EU share historic ties and there is a need for further improvement. In the new changing world order, India-EU relations can grow but there is a need to shift the focus from trade ties to geostrategic issues. There have been functional areas of Indo-EU cooperation as diverse as renewable energy to counter-terrorism. The India-EU cooperation is yet to gain the momentum needed to actualize this strategic functional partnership. The signing of bilateral trade and investment agreement is an immediate roadblock for boosting trade ties between India and the EU. The misconstrued perceptions as noted above are the basic constraints in realizing the BTIA. The time has come for India to understand EU as a whole and its importance as a global actor. The strength of relations with the member states of EU may be considered as one of the ways of reinforcing the relationship with the institutions of EU.

Endnotes

1. Common, shared and mutual interests and commitments between India and EU are often reiterated at the conclusion of the annual summits through joint statements and press releases. It is a point of debate, however, in regard to the substance of those interests particularly in matters of security. The remarks of former PM were at the India-EU Summit in Marseille, France on September 29, 2008.
2. Inter-governmentalism as a term was proposed by Stanley Hoffman that refers to a theory of regional integration which treats states and national governments as primary factors for integration. Supranationalism refers to delegation of certain competences of decision-making to a body higher/above the State for purposes of integration.
3. It is one among the several tasks of European External Action Service (EEAS) to represent the voice of Europe internationally.
4. David Allen, "The EU and India: Strategic Partners but not a Strategic Partnership" in Thomas Christiansen (ed.), 'The Palgrave Handbook of EU Asia Relations', Basingstoke: Palgrave, 2013.
5. In ancient Greece, a general often functioned as a magistrate with political influence and wider powers. Cliesthenes bought in 10 strategi in Athens to be commanders of the army; all are equally responsible for each operation.
6. For definitions see: "The International Relations Dictionary", New York, Holt, Reinhart and Winston, 1969, p. 127; Joseph Frankel, "The Making of Foreign Policy: An Analysis of Decision-making", London: Oxford University Press, 1967, p. 1;

and Frederick H. Hartmann, "The Relations of Nations", New York: Macmillan, 1978, p. 69.

7. A.P. Rana, "The Imperatives of Non-alignment: A Conceptual Study of India's Foreign Policy Strategy in the Nehru Period", New Delhi: Macmillan, 1976 pp. 2-3.
8. Professor Taylor as quoted by Raghubir Chakraborti cited in "International Relations", Calcutta: The World Press Pvt. Ltd., 1970, p. 228.
9. Ibid., p. 228.
10. See Raghubir Chakraborti cited in, "International Relations", Calcutta: The World Press Pvt. Ltd., 1970, p. 229.
11. Mahendra Kumar, "Theoretical Aspects of International Politics", Agra: Shivlal Agarwala & Company, 1993, p. 322.
12. H.J. Morgenthau as quoted by A. Appadorai in, "Essays in Politics and International Relations", Bombay: Asian Publishing House, 1969, p. 168.
13. See Mahendra Kumar, "Theoretical Aspects of International Politics", Agra: Shivlal Agarwala & Company, 1993, p. 325.
14. Umma Salma Bawa, "The EU as a Security Actor", pp. 98-106 in Rajendra K. Jain (ed.), 'India and the EU: Building a Strategic Partnership', New Delhi: Radiant Publishers, 2007.
15. The term civilian power was coined by Francois Duchene. For details, see, Francois Duchene, "The European Community and the Uncertainties of Independence" in Max Kohnstam and Wolfgang Hager (eds.), 'A Nation Writ large? Foreign Policy Problems before the European Community', London: Macmillan, 1973, p. 19.
16. C.O. Meyer, "Theorizing European Strategic Culture: Between Convergences and the Persistence of National Diversity", Working Document No. 204, Brussels: Centre for European Policy Studies, 2004.
17. Council of European Union, "A Secure Europe in a Better World: The European Security Strategy", December 12, 2003, Brussels: European Institute for Security Studies, p. 21.
18. Ibid.
19. Dr. Javier Solana, the High Representative for Common and Foreign Security in an interview to Xinhua News Agency, China Youth Daily, March 17, 2004.
20. Ibid.
21. Comment by then Minister of Commerce and Industry, India

cited in "India and USA: Equal Partners", *Economic Times Supplement*, March 2, 2006, p. 1.

22. European External Action Service (EEAS), Joint Press Statement for 5th India-EU Summit, The Hague: Netherlands, November 8, 2004.
23. Gauri Khandekar, "The EU and India: A Loveless Arranged Marriage", Policy Brief, *FRIDE*, No. 90, August 2011.
24. Christopher Jafferlot, "India and European Union: The Charade of a Strategic Partnership", *CERI-Science PO/CNRS*, March 2006.
25. Harsh V. Pant, "India and the EU: A Directionless Courtship", Rediff.com, October 7, 2008.
26. Kristy Hughes, "EU India: Blossoming Partnership or Strategic Irrelevance?", *Economic and Political Weekly*, Vol. XL, No. 41, October 8, 2005.
27. Rajendra K. Jain, "India and Europe in the New Millennium", New Delhi: Radiant Publishers, 2001.
28. Bernd von Muenchow-Pohl, "India and Europe in a Multipolar World", The Carnegie Papers, Carnegie Endowment for International Peace, Washington, 2012.
29. Gauri Khandekar, "The EU-India Summit: On the Threshold of Change", ESP, European Strategic Partnerships Observatory, Policy Brief 1, Brussels, February 2012.
30. Bharti Chibber, "India-EU Economic Relations: FTA in the Offing", *Mainstream Weekly,* Vol. L, No. 30, July 14, 2012.
31. Rajendra K. Jain, "India's Relations with the European Union" in David Scott (ed.), 'India's Foreign Relations', Routledge, 2012, pp. 223-233. Also see: R. Pandey, "The European Union in the Eyes of India", *Asia Europe Journal*, 8, 2010, 193-209.
32. Manu Pubby, "PM Narendra Modi's Brussels Visit Cancelled as EU Fails to Respond", *Economic Times*, March 15, 2015, available at: http://articles.economictimes.indiatimes.com/2015-03-14/news/60111638_1_italian-marines-india-european-union-suggestions.
33. "EU Projects to Bridge Digital Divide", Express News Service, February 18, 2015.

References

Appadorai, A. (1969), "Essays in Politics and International

Relations", Bombay: Asian Publishing House.

Chakraborti, Raghubir (1970), "International Relations", Calcutta: The World Press Pvt. Ltd.

Christiansen, Thomas, Emil Kirchner, Philomena B. Murray (eds.) (2013), "The Palgrave Handbook of EU-Asia Relations", Basingstoke: Palgrave.

Chibber, Bharti (2012) "India-EU Economic Relations: FTA in the Offing", *Mainstream,* Vol. L, No. 30, July 14.

Frankel, Joseph (1967), "The Making of Foreign Policy: An Analysis of Decision-making", London: Oxford University Press.

Hartmann, Frederick H. (1978), "The Relations of Nations", New York: Macmillan.

Hughes, Kristy (2005), "EU-India: Blossoming Partnership or Strategic Irrelevance?", *Economic and Political Weekly*, Vol. XL, No. 41, October 8.

Jain, Rajendra K. (2001), "India and Europe in the New Millennium", New Delhi: Radiant Publishers.

Jain, Rajendra K. (ed.) (2007), "India and the European Union: Building a Strategic Partnership", New Delhi: Radiant Publishers.

Jain, R. Pandey (2010), "The European Union in the Eyes of India", *Asia Europe Journal*, 8: 193-209.

Jafferlot, Christopher (2006), "India and European Union: The Charade of a Strategic Partnership", *CERI-Science PO/CNRS*, March.

Khandekar, Gauri (2011), "The EU and India: A Loveless Arranged Marriage", Policy Brief, FRIDE, No. 90, August.

Khandekar, Gauri (2012), "The EU-India Summit: On the Threshold of Change", ESP, European Strategic Partnerships Observatory, Policy Brief 1, Brussels, February.

Kumar, Mahendra (1993), "Theoretical Aspects of International Politics", Agra: Shivlal Agarwala & Company.

Kohnstam, Max and Wolfgang Hager (eds.) (1973), "A Nation Writ Large? Foreign Policy Problems before the European Community", London: Macmillan.

Meyer, C.O. (2004), "Theorizing European Strategic Culture: Between Convergences and the Persistence of National Diversity", Working Document No. 204, Brussels: Centre for European Policy Studies.

McLean, Iain and Alistair McMillan (eds.) (2004), "The Concise

Oxford Dictionary of Politics", New Delhi: Oxford University Press.

Muenchow-Pohl, Bernd von (2012), "India and Europe in a Multipolar World", The Carnegie Papers, Washington: Carnegie Endowment for International Peace.

Rana, A.P. (1976), "The Imperatives of Non-alignment: A Conceptual Study of India's Foreign Policy Strategy in the Nehru Period", New Delhi: Macmillan.

Pant, Harsh V. (2008), "India and the EU: A Directionless Courtship", Rediff.com, October 7.

Pappas, Theodore (ed.) (2005), "Britannica Ready Reference Encyclopaedia", New Delhi.

Scott, David (ed.) (2012), "Handbook of India's International Relations", London and New York: Routledge.

7

India-Russia Relations in the Emerging World Order

K.B. Usha

India and Russia have emerged as vital strategic partners representing global transformation from a unipolar world order dominated by one centre to a multipolar order based on multilateralism, principles of UN Charter, non-intervention, cooperation, convergence of national interests, mutual understanding and trust. This is because of the perceived failures of the American "unipolar movement", which is guided by the principles of pre-emptive strikes, regime change, disarmament and intervention. After twenty-five years of Soviet disintegration, the current geopolitical realities like rift in the US-Russia-Europe relations over Ukraine conflict, global oil crisis, economic crisis, Euro zone crisis, conflict in West Asia, NATO military build-up and expansion to Russia's border, escalation of terrorist attacks in Europe, emergence of BRICS countries, Russia's shifting priorities to Asia-Pacific, commencement of Eurasian Economic Union, and shifting power alignments from West to East expose the dangers of unilateralism and reflect a paradigm shift in the world order.

In the changing global scenario, Russia has re-emerged as an independent player on the world scene and India attained the reputation of an emerging global economic power next to China. India-Russia relations, which existed as time-tested since the Soviet days based on convergence of national interests, mutual trust, confidence and understanding, have been depicting a long-term synergy, especially since the signing of "Declaration on the India-Russia Strategic

Partnership" in October 2000 during the visit of President Putin to India.

Thereafter, relations have been qualitatively transformed in virtually all areas such as defence, energy, technology and innovation, global issues and order, and has revitalised economic cooperation and elevated the partnership to the level of a "Special and Privileged Strategic Partnership". The new government that came to power in India in May 2014 also asserted Russia's unique place in Indian foreign policy and is determined to look for strengthening the India-Russia relations over the next decade. In short, Russia remains a strong pillar in India's foreign policy matrix and the bilateral relations are in the core interests of both the countries, although certain regional political issues stand as challenges. This paper is an attempt to examine the present state of India-Russia relations, its significance in the emerging world order, and the challenges, issues and opportunities way ahead.

Global Strategic Context

The collapse of Berlin wall in 1989 and the disintegration of Soviet Union in 1991 led to an end of the bipolar system and Cold War and marked the beginning of a new phase in the global order. [1] As a result of globalization, states are weakened and their traditional social role and intensified corporatization at the cost of nature and human lives is a major challenge for people all over the world (Bhambhri, 1997). New forms of authorities and multiple actors—state, non-state, transnational and intergovernmental—have emerged and continue to emerge in the international system challenging the earlier established forms of authority.

Disintegration of Soviet Union created a global order in terms of polarity, a "unipolar moment". The triumphalist US political elites did not satisfy with containment of Soviet Union. In the post-Soviet period, they targeted continuously Russia in their pursuit of global hegemon. Robert Gates, referring to Dick Cheney, former US Defence Secretary and

Vice President, wrote in his memoir, Duty: Memoirs of a Secretary at War, "When the Soviet Union was collapsing in late 1991, Dick wanted to see the dismantlement not only of the Soviet Union and the Russian empire but of Russia itself, so it could never again be a threat to the rest of the world" (Gates, 2014).

His statement undoubtedly clarifies why Euro-American imperialists are after Russia and reveals that the underpinnings of the US policy in Eurasia had the goal of complete destruction of Russia. Such a goal is further evident in US policy of sanctions on Russia and Russophobia in the context of Ukraine crisis with the aim to economically weaken and politically isolate so as to foment a "regime change" in Russia and install an American puppet Government there. With the depiction of "Russia as an aggressor", the US and West made it clear that they view Russia as a "threat to global security", on which logic, NATO continues its military expansion near Russia's borders. Russia at present is confronting containment II policy of the West.

The US "pivot to Asia" is another containment policy in the Asian region to prevent the rise of China, challenging American economic power in the global stage. In preventing China, the US political elites see India as a counterweight to be used against China. According to Henry Kissinger, former US State Secretary, "India will be a fulcrum of twenty-first century order: an indispensable element, based on its geography, resources, and tradition of sophisticated leadership, in the strategic and ideological equation of the region and of the global order at whose interaction it stands" (Kissinger, 2014).

It is in this global context that Russia is calling for a multipolar world order and a consensus of responsible powers that respect international law and sovereignty of other states. Putin is trying to develop close strategic alliance and partnership with countries like China, India, Turkey, Egypt, etc., and through Eurasian integration, and platforms like BRICS, SCO and G20.

When resurgent Russia, rising China and emerging India come close, this alliance projects a shift in power alignment in the eastern direction. Vladimir Putin maintains that such an alliance might counter NATO expansion and neo-liberal capitalism and strengthen multipolarity. He believes that Russia, China and India together can ensure the emergence of a multipolar world order which will be more democratic, equitable, prosperous and peaceful.

In an interview given to Indian media and Russian RTR TV channel on the eve of Putin's India visit in 2000 to their question as to what factors have contributed to the strategic alliance between Russia and India, Putin replied:

"India, in my opinion, is a key factor in world politics, not only in regional politics but, I stress, in world politics. And we are interested in maintaining relations with such a great power as India in pursuing the goals that we seek to achieve internationally: stabilisation and the creation of a modern democratic world order, and the goals that we set in bilateral relations. Russia and India are also natural partners in terms of their mutually complementary economic, scientific and technological potential" (Putin, 2000).

Here, it is clear that Russia wants a long-term partnership with India based on the recognition of sovereignty, territorial integrity and convergence of each other's legitimate interests.

Indian foreign policy of non-alignment takes a new meaning in the changing situations. Multilateral alliances and strategic autonomy are the two principles apart from national interest included in India's foreign policy. India showed support to Russia on the Crimean issue. India does not support the US containment and isolationist measures against countries like Russia, China, Iran and Burma but continues to maintain diplomatic relationship. India ignored Obama's advice that "it is not a good time to do business with Russia" when he visited India as a chief guest during the Republic Day celebrations on January 26, 2015. It shows that India and Russia have a lot of opportunities to work together in the changed global scenario.

Historical Background

India-Russia relations predate India's Independence. It is a general understanding that India-Russia relations have the uniqueness of civilizational basis and deep historical roots, mutual understanding and convergence of interests. J.A. Naik notes that Russian accounts indicate the existence of economic and cultural contacts between the two peoples much before the October Revolution and British conquest of India. The first Russian writing on India appeared in 12th-13th century known as "The Relation about India" or "The Story of India, the Rich" (Naik, 1995: 1).

Russian mercantile Diaspora, travellers and Indologists also gave accounts about India. Russian merchant from the city of Tver, Afanasy Nikitin visited India in the 15th century (1446-1472) and published accounts of his travel. His work *Beyond Three Seas* (*Khozhdenieza tri moria*) is considered as the first eyewitness account of India by a Russian. Gerasim Lebedev, a Russian traveller reached India in 1785. He was a creative intellectual who possessed expertise in music, drama, Sanskrit and the Bengali language. He was considered the first Russian Indologist (Naik, 1995).

By 17th century a large number Indian traders were settled in Astrakhan in the Volga Basin. They developed contacts with Moscow and St. Petersburg even during the days of Peter the great. The Tsarist government even granted temporary citizenship with equivalent rights and duties enjoyed by the Russian merchants (Naik, 1995). During the years of war against Napoleon in 1812, the Indian merchants generously contributed to the Russian victory. Over two and a half centuries ago, Peter the Great sent his special envoy Vice Admiral D. Wilster to India to sign an agreement, to "work as hard as possible in order to have fruitful commercial relations between the two sides" (Vajpayee, 2000; Kaushik, 1971).

Mahatma Gandhi was highly influenced by Leo Tolstoy in experiments with truth and non-violence and developing his non-violent resistance, *Satyagraha*, in Indian freedom struggle.

Tolstoy's famous "letter to a Hindoo" attracted Gandhi (Anand, 2010). "Kalidasa, Prem Chand and Krishan Chander were as popular in Russia as were Tolstoy, Gorky, Pushkin and Dostoevsky in India. The famous Russian historian Nikolai Karamzin said about Kalidas' works, "for me Kalidasa is no less important than Homer". Generations of Russians danced to the tune of "Awara Hun" and Indians exulted in the excellence of Anna Pavlova's art. This is only a small glimpse of the size and the splendour of the Indo-Russian civilizational relations" (Kant, 2000).

Jawaharlal Nehru was deeply impressed by Soviet economic planning. His fascination to Soviet model of development and socialism led to the India's "socialistic pattern of development" and close strategic relation with the Soviet Union. Upon Nehru's proposal for establishing diplomatic relations, Soviet Union began diplomatic relations with India on April 13, 1947, six months before she gained Independence (Pant, 2013).

The Indo-Soviet Treaty of Peace, Friendship and Cooperation in 1971 was another landmark event in the relation between the two countries (Imam, 1987). The significance of this Treaty is reflected in the words of K.P.S. Menon: "I have never known a measure which was greeted with such a widespread enthusiasm by my countrymen as the Indo-Soviet Treaty of Peace, Friendship and Cooperation. The immediate reaction was one of instantaneous relief. It was as if one has been walking alone through a dark forest infested with snakes and robbers and suddenly emerged into a sunlit glade" (quoted in Sahai, 1990: 12; Menon, 1971).

Soviet President Mikhail Gorbachev's visit to India in November 1986 and the signing of 10 point Delhi declaration by Indian Prime Minister Rajiv Gandhi and Gorbachev on principles of nuclear weapons-free and non-violent world was a historical event in Indo-Soviet relations (Subrahmanyam, 1987). In his interface with the journalists in India, Gorbachev said that "Lenin was guided by respect for Indian people, when he insightfully predicted India's important role in international affairs. The idea of Lenin motivated our policies and actions in regard to India. Many generations of Soviet and Indian leaders have worked hard so that we might see our relations in such a state today" (Subrahmanyam, 1987: 37; Sahai, 1990: 5).

The basic principles for which India and Soviet Union stood for were articulated in the Delhi Declaration of 1986 in defence of humanity and stand relevant even today after twenty-five years of the disintegration of the Soviet Union. The principles were: "(a) Peaceful co-existence must become the universal norm of international relations; (b) Human life must be recognized as supreme; (c) Non-violence should be the basis of community life; (d) Understanding and trust must replace fear and suspicion; (e) The right of every state to political and economic independence must be recognized and respected; (f) Resources being spent on armaments must be channelled towards social and economic development; (g) Conditions must be guaranteed for individuals' harmonious development; (h) Mankind's material and intellectual potential must be used to solve global problems; (i) The 'balance of terror' must give way to international security; (j) A nuclear weapon-free and non-violent world requires specific and immediate action for disarmament" (Sahai: 17-18).

Rajiv Gandhi emphasized that Delhi declaration is a historic document which embodies a comprehensive new framework for international relations based on freedom, equality and non-violence and is a major contribution to a cooperative and peaceful world order. Its international significance will be seen in time (Ibid: 22).

India-Russia Relations in the Post-Bipolar World

The Soviet disintegration was a great shock to India and left her with uncertainty and chaos in the initial years. Russia was preoccupied with economic recovery. Boris Yeltsin who was President followed Atlanticist pro-Western policies. Atlanticists were not interested in developing relations with

India. Therefore, there was a neglect of India in the initial years, i.e., during 1991-1993 by Russia. Gradually, Russian leadership understood that the US and West were not treating Russia as an equal partner, but they expect Russia to be a junior partner. Russians believed that they, like any other great power, should develop a diverse foreign policy cultivating strong ties with both the West and with China, India, Japan and countries of the Far East and Middle East (Belopolsky, 2009: 20).

When Vladimir Putin became President in 2000 he asserted Eurasianist foreign policy based on maximising Russian interests through aligning with both East and the West. He visited India on October 2-5, 2000. President Putin and Prime Minister Vajpayee jointly signed Declaration for Strategic Partnership between India and Russia and launched the annual Summit process in New Delhi in October 2000. Delhi Declaration became the foundation for new relations between India and Russia and Putin became the architect of India-Russia relations in the 21st century. This Declaration was a continuation of earlier treaties from 1971 Treaty of Friendship and Cooperation, to Moscow Declaration of June 1994.

During the visit, Putin visited Bhabha Atomic Research Centre (BARC) in Mumbai on October 5, 2000 (BARC 2000). He was the first Russian leader to visit BARC. He also visited Jawaharlal Nehru University in New Delhi where the world's biggest centre of Russian Studies is located. He was honoured with the title of honorary doctor of law. In his speech Putin stated, "India is a reliable ally of Russia" (kremlin.ru, 2000). He also attended a lunch hosted in honour by the then President of India Kocheril Raman Narayanan. Speaking at the lunch Putin called signing of Delhi Declaration as "an important milestone in the two country's bilateral relations" (kremlin.ru, 2000).

The significance of this Declaration is that it was signed in the global and regional context of unipolarity, US domination, regional political instability (Afghanistan) and security threats (cross border terrorism) which are common for both India and Russia. The framework of annual summits, guiding principles and commitments were shaped in the Delhi Declaration as the basis for future trajectory of bilateral partnership in the 21st century. Both countries set up a Joint Working Group on Afghanistan, an Inter-Governmental Commission for Military Technical Cooperation, and a process for active cooperation between the National Security Council of India and the Security Council of the Russian Federation, election commission of the two countries, Comptroller and Auditors General of India and Russia, and the judicial authorities of the two countries. The Integrated Long Term Programme Cooperation in Space and Technology was extended for ten years until 2010 (MEA, 2000).

In the second summit held in Moscow in November 2001, in the atmosphere of terrorist attacks in US on September 11, 2001 and the US-declared war on terror, the focus was on international terrorism and insurgency. The summit condemned Pakistan's help to cross border terrorism and support to Kashmiri militants in India and Taliban in Afghanistan. In the third summit in 2002, the two sides unveiled "Delhi Declaration on Further Consolidation of Strategic Partnership". The fourth summit in 2003 held after the US invasion in Iraq, clearly stressed the dangers of American unilateralism and emphasised the common position that the future world order should be "based on multipolarity" and "should be determined by collective and multilateral processes rather than unilateral ones" (Embassy of Russian Federation in the Republic of India, 2003). India expressed its full support to Russia's membership in WTO. The first Indo-Russian Inter-Ministerial Consultations on economic issues and the World Trade Organization was held in March 2003 in New Delhi (Nadkarni, 2010).

The 2004 summit at the background of India's enhanced strategic partnership with the US was titled "Next Steps in the Strategic Partnership". Russia had concerns about the defence cooperation. India confirmed significance of partnership with

Russia reaffirming India's support to Russia's early entry into WTO. India's strengthening relations with the US was viewed with concern in Russia. Russia viewed it as India's tilt towards the Western orbit (Embassy of Russian Federation in the Republic of India, 2004). During the 2005 summit meeting, Pranab Mukherji cleared the doubts saying that "India is the largest importer of military equipment, platforms, arms and systems from Russia. This cooperation is set to expand in the future. There is no danger of our cooperation in the area weakening" (quoted in Nadkarni, 2010: 93).

India understood the need for neutralising India-Russia ties at the summit held in January 2007 in New Delhi. President was invited as the chief guest in the Republic Day celebrations. Indian side called the ties "tension-free" as Russia did not "create problems" for India in its neighbourhood. Russian side addressed Indian concerns over the Chinese supply of fighter aircraft equipped with Russian engines to Pakistan "by invoking the end user provisions in its agreement with China to prevent this from happening" (Subrahmanyam quoted in Ibid: 94).

In the 2008 summit, the relations seemed to have stabilized as Medvedev emphasised that relations with India are of "utmost importance" to Russia. Besides joint declaration, nine agreements of cooperation on priority areas were signed. Three important agreements were: Inter-Governmental Agreement on Cooperation in the construction of additional nuclear power plant units at Kudankulamand, construction of Russian designed nuclear power plants at new sites and a MoU between ISRO and Russian Federal Space Agency on joint activities in the field of human space flight programme (MEA, 2009).

In the 2009 summit held in Moscow, the Prime Minister's visit for bilateral cooperation in key areas such as defence, space research, science and technology, and energy security (including hydrocarbons and nuclear energy) intensified (MEA, 2010). Eleventh summit held in 2010 in New Delhi reviewed the partnership of the decade and elevated to a high level.

From Friendship to "Special and Privileged" Strategic Partnership

In the eleventh annual India-Russia summit in 2010, India-Russia relations had been elevated to "Special and Privileged Strategic Partnership" in 2010 (MEA, 2011). Former Prime Minister Manmohan Singh stated that "The tradition of annual summits with Russia symbolises the richness of our relationship with Russia. Russia is a time-tested friend of India that has stood by us in our times of need in the past...Ours is a very special and privileged strategic partnership. It is a partnership that has and will continue to develop independently of our relations with other countries" (Singh, 2010).

15th Summit and *Druzhba-Dosti* Vision: Roadmap of Future Co-operation

Russia, as India's 'special and privileged' strategic partner, continues to occupy an important place in India's foreign policy priorities. Bilateral relations with Russia struck a high note with the successful visit of President Putin to India for the 15th Annual Summit in December 2014. During the visit, the Russian President and Prime Minister Shri Narendra Modi outlined an ambitious vision of bilateral cooperation expected to guide the future relationship. In the summit, twenty agreements and commercial contracts were signed in key areas such as defence, energy and space, nuclear energy, technology and innovation, fertilizers, diamonds, expansion in economic engagement, business, culture, and people to people contact.

Besides these, other potential areas were also mentioned to enhance cooperation in pharmaceuticals, diamond industry, IT sector, clean energy, etc. A range of regional and global issues which affect Russia and India directly and indirectly such as international terrorism, militancy, Afghanistan and foreign support to militants were specified to be addressed jointly. The new projects in both government and private sectors were signs of enhancement in the current status of bilateral cooperation.

In India's defence sector, Russia has dominated and cooperation has grown from a consumer-supplier relation to joint projects and collaboration. India and Russia have joint military programmes like BarhMos, fifth generation fighter Sukhoi, etc. Production of Sukhoi Superjet-100 and MS-21passenger aircraft in India is under discussion. INS Vikramaditya, the aircraft carrier purchased by India in 2004 was inducted into the Indian navy by PM Modi and dedicated to the nation in June 2014 (MEA, 2014).

In the energy sector, cooperation in joint nuclear energy projects aims at serial construction of nuclear power units, based on Russian design. Construction of more reactors at Kudankulam nuclear plant and at new sites is agreed. India has invested US$ 2.8 billion in the Sakhalin-1 project and purchased Imperial Energy, the London-listed oil major in the Tomsk region. India has decided to start new acquisitions in Vankor oilfield (East Siberia) and Timan Pechora basin (Northeast European Russia) and to launch joint exploration in the Arctic (MEA, 2014). Russia and India are looking to forge and develop cooperation in space monitoring and in the field of training forces to respond to emergency situations (Russia and India Report, 2015).

Technology and innovation, information and communication technologies, nanotechnology, engineering science, bio-energy, nano-biotechnology, bio-equipment and affordable diagnosing equipment for healthcare and agriculture are other areas of cooperation. India-Russia trade basket was only US$ 9.5 billion in 2014. It is expected that Russian companies will utilize the opportunities in a wide range of Indian sectors under the 'Make in India' programme. The economic sector targets a trade level of US$ 30 billion and investments in total by 2025 (MEA, 2015). The sides will encourage cooperation to promote health and fitness through traditional Indian forms of yoga and ayurveda, including through yoga centres, camps and ayurveda centres (MEA,

2014). Indian private sector companies have also begun investing in Russia.

Both the countries are concerned about terrorist acts that have recently happened in Jammu & Kashmir, India and in Chechnya, Russia. The sides agreed to work together for the adoption of the Comprehensive Convention on International Terrorism by the 70th Anniversary Summit of the UN. The leaders expressed hope that terrorism would be completely eradicated from the common region within a decade (MEA, 2014). India and Russia had welcomed the peaceful transition of political authority in Afghanistan and called upon the international community to join efforts to support reconstruction and economic development in that country and to continue capacity building of its national security forces. The Russian side confirmed its support to India's intention to seek full membership in the Nuclear Suppliers Group, Missile Technology Control Regime (MTCR) and Wassenaar Arrangement (MEA, 2014).

Modi's Russia Policy: Pragmatism, Strategic Autonomy and Continuity

The 15th India-Russia annual summit and Modi's approach to Russia remains a test of India's strategic autonomy, pragmatism and continuity in foreign policy. Some analysts say that the vision "India First" is both ideology and pragmatism in Modi's foreign policy. India's civilizational grace is also important for him. He is showing a very committed focus on India's development in principle through his "Make in India" drive.

Modi asserted the importance of Russia that India attached to her relations with Russia despite the pressure the US tried to put on India during President Putin's visit to New Delhi. His statements amply prove his foreign policy independence. During Putin's visit to India, the US State Department spokesperson Jen Psaki said, "Our view remains that it's not time for business as usual with Russia. But beyond that, we'd have to take a closer look at what these agreements entail"

(Psaki quoted in Haider, 2014). This was an atmosphere of warning that America tried to impose on India. India's Ministry of External Affairs refused to comment on US pressure, but Indian Ambassador to Russia, P.S. Raghavan made it very clear that "There is no question of India being pressurized by any country to change its behaviour towards Russia or to change its attitude towards anything that concerns India-Russia relations" (quoted in Upadhyay, 2014).

On the sidelines of BRICS summit in Fortaleza, Prime Minister Modi said: "Every child in India knows that Russia is our best friend" (quoted in Mohanty, 2014). The Prime Minister "reaffirmed that relations with Russia will continue to enjoy the priority that they always had in India's foreign policy and that he looks forward to working with President Putin to further deepen and broad base the strategic partnership including in the areas of defence, nuclear energy, space, energy, trade and investment, people-to-people contacts and addressing regional and global challenges" (Press Information Bureau, 2014a).

On refusal to condemn Russia's annexation of Crimea, Modi said hinting US policy: "In the world right now, a lot of people want to give us advice. But look within them, they too have sinned" (Zakaria, 2014). Modi said: "President Putin is a leader of a great nation with which we have a friendship of unmatched mutual confidence, trust and goodwill. We have a strategic partnership that is incomparable in content. The character of global politics and international relations is changing. However, the importance of this relationship and its unique position in India's foreign policy will not change. In many ways its significance to both countries will grow further in future. President Putin and I agreed that this is a challenging moment in the world. Our partnership and strong sensitivity that we have always had for each other's interests will be a source of strength to both the countries" (News Nation Bureau, 2014). Modi tweeted on December 11, 2014, "Wonderful day with President Putin. Our meeting was comprehensive. India's partnership with Russia is incomparable" (Modi, 2014).

Moreover, the joint Summit Declaration signed by Putin and Modi clearly stated that "India and Russia oppose economic sanctions that do not have the approval of the United Nations Security Council" (Press Information Bureau, 2014b). Modi's above statements are evident enough to show his determination to keep relationship with Russia on high priority.

Continuing India's special relationship with Russia, the new government established contacts with Russia immediately after assuming office. Prime Minister Shri Narendra Modi met President Mr. Vladimir Putin on the sidelines of the Summit in Brazil (July 2014), followed by a bilateral meeting on the sidelines of the G-20 Summit in Australia (November 2014). Prime Minister Shri Narendra Modi also met Russian Prime Minister Mr. Dmitry Medvedev in Myanmar on the sidelines of the East Asia Summit held in November 2014. Fifteenth annual India-Russia Summit is another milestone for taking the time-tested, all weather, special and privileged strategic partnership to new heights as the *Druzhba-Dosti* joint declaration demonstrates. No spectacle of change or paradigm shift is present at the moment.

Conclusion

The India-Russia relation is evolving in the global and regional strategic contexts characterized by unipolarity, guided by American primacy principles, NATO's eastward expansion and terrorism. Political volatility in Afghanistan, Kashmir and Chechnya issues, and Western containment policy II against Russia have implications for international security and Eurasian region. India and Russia view the above factors as dangerous trends and threat to global peace, stability and security. Both India and Russia challenge unipolarity and call for a new, equitable, democratic, peaceful and just multipolar world order, conducive for human development and prosperity. In this context, India-Russia strategic partnership, which has a firm foundation based on deep rooted historical and civilizational affinities, mutual trust and confidence, convergence of interests and common perception on global issues, has global significance. India, an emerging global economic power and Russia, a rising great power in her struggle to consolidate independence and sovereignty confronting Western sanctions and other humiliating punitive policies, are committed to improve the world.

After a short-lived neglect by Russia in the initial years until 1993, Russia began to reconsider upgrading relations with India. By 2000, when Vladimir Putin became President of the Russian Federation, his constructive and pragmatic foreign policy determined to reconcile Russia's "loss of position in India". India welcomed that change in Russia's policy wholeheartedly to mark the amity in future course of Indo-Russian relations. India responded to Russia's partnership initiatives positively and set the stage for bringing back the old Soviet era warmth in bilateral cooperation.

Both countries have held as of now, 15 annual summits alternatively in New Delhi and Moscow, and strengthened cooperation in defence, energy, trade, science and technology, space research, culture, tourism and in the process enhanced cooperation in potential areas like pharmaceuticals, tourism and education. Putin's visit in 2014 for the India-Russia Summit, signing of agreements and joint declaration by Narendra Modi and Vladimir Putin demonstrate that India-Russia relations will continue without any major constraints. Cooperation will continue over the coming years looking forward to make this world better, safer, more prosperous and multipolar. Several unsettled global and regional issues of strategic importance for both countries exist such as Afghanistan, Kashmir question, Ukraine, terrorism, and so on.

Although India-Russia relations are qualified as unique and time tested, at times short lived irritants appeared in India-Russia relations. After the disintegration of Soviet Union, the position of the then Russian leadership was not in favour of developing a special relationship with India. In 1998, when India conducted nuclear tests without informing Russia,

President Yeltsin sent a message to India that she could not take it for granted. India's ties with the US were likely to have an indirect impact on her relations with Russia. Likewise, India had discontent with Russia's approach to Pakistan and China.

In 2004, India's tilt towards the US was not well taken by the Russian leadership and they expressed their dissatisfaction on such a policy harming the Russian interests. Since 2005, Russia resented to India's cooperation with the US in missile defence and participation in quadrilateral military exercise. As India is a big market for Russian armaments, Russia does not want others to dominate in this field. But both countries are diversifying their market. This shows that bilateral relations have only a strong foundation, but this does not mean that either partner takes the relations for granted. Economic relations are the weakest link in India-Russia relations.

In the way ahead, several questions remain to be addressed for tapping the full potential of the relationship in the changing context of global politics and world order. Why does at present India-Russia relations remain less rich in content and limited mainly to defence and energy cooperation? Why haven't the trade and commercial relations between India and Russia taken off? Whether the improved India-US ties impinge on India's relation with Russia? Whether Russia's arms trade with Pakistan will have adverse implications on India-Russia relations? Whether China's rise in the Asian region and her relations with Pakistan has implications for India-Russia relations? How does the Russia-China strategic partnership influence India-Russia relations in the changing global and regional geopolitical situation? What has to be done to enrich the content of India-Russia relations in future?

In the emerging global context, if the relations should continue friction-free—as former Indian Vice President Krishna Kant qualifies it, as the waters of *Ganga* and *Volga*, the "great rivers represent two great civilizations and their perennial flow symbolises the permanence, the serenity and the continuity of our contacts"—much has to be done by both the sides to cement the relationship further ahead in the coming years.

Endnote

1. The emerging world order is considered as the third phase in terms of polarity in the new world order created after the end of Second World War. In the first phase, the world order was bipolar. Bloc politics based on two opposing ideologies of socialism/communism and capitalism, military deterrence and Cold War were the perceived characteristics in the world order during this phase. Soviet Union led the socialist bloc and the US with its European allies led the capitalist bloc with containment of communism in Soviet Union as one of its major foreign policy priorities.

References

Anand, Y.P. (2010), "The Relationship between Leo Tolstoy and Mahatma Gandhi: A Historical Review", *Dialogue*, Vol. 12, No. 2, October-December 2010.

BARC, "Russian President Visits BARC", available at: http://www.barc.gov.in/publications/nl/2000/200012-04.pdf.

Belopolsky, Helen (2009), "Russia and the Challengers: Russian Alignment with China, Iran and Iraq in the Unipolar Era", London: Palgrave Macmillan.

Bhambhri, C.P. (2005), "Globalization and India: Nation, State and Democracy", New Delhi: Shipra Publications.

Embassy of Russian Federation in the Republic of India (2003), "Declaration of the Russian Federation and the Republic of India on Global Challenges and Threats to World Security and Stability", November 12, 2003, available at: http://rusembindia.com/russia-india-dialogue-en/official-documents/120officialdocuments/1757-declaration-of-the-russian-federation-and-the-republic-of-india-on-global-challenges-and-threats-to-world-security-and stability-12-november-2003.

Embassy of Russian Federation in the Republic of India (2004), "Joint declaration by the Russian Federation and the Republic of India," December 3, 2004, available at: http://rusembindia.com/russia-india-dialogue-en/120-

officialdocuments/1760-joint-declaration-by-the-russian-federation-and-the-republic-of-india-3-december-2004.

Embassy of Russian Federation (2013), "Russian-Indian relations are on the rise: Kadakin on Rajya Sabha TV", October 31, 2013, available at: http://in.rbth.com/economics/2013/10/31/russian-indian_relations_are_on_the_rise_kadakin_on_rajya_sabha_tv_30489.html.

Haider, Suhasini (2014), "U.S. Upset at India-Russia Deals", *The Hindu*, New Delhi, December 13, 2014, available at: http://www.thehindu.com/news/national/us-upset-at-indiarussia-deals-says-cant-be-business-as-usual/article6686903.ece.

HT Correspondent (2015), "Modi's Foreign Policy Better Than UPA's, says Shivshankar Menon", *Hindustan Times*, New Delhi, March 17, 2015, available at: http://www.hindustantimes.com/india-news/modi-s-foreign-policy-better-than-upa-s-says-shivshankar-menon/article1-1327152.aspx.

Imama, Zafar (ed.) (1983), "Towards a Model Relationship: A Study of Soviet Theatre with India and other Third World Countries", New Delhi: ABC Publishing House.

Kant, Krishna (2000), "Vice-President of India and Chairman, Rajya Sabha, Address in Parliament of India", available at: http://parliamentofindia.nic.in/jpi/December2000/CHAP-1.htm.

Kaushik, Devendra (1971), "Soviet Relation with India and Pakistan", Delhi: Vikas Publications.

Kissinger, Henry (2014), "World Order", New York: Penguin Press.

Kremlin.ru (2000), "President Vladimir Putin visited Jawaharlal Nehru University", October 3, 2000, available at: http://en.kremlin.ru/events/president/news/39451.

Kremlin.ru (2000), "President Vladimir Putin Attended a Lunch Hosted in his Honour by President of India Kocheril Raman Narayanan", October 3, 2000, available at: http://en.kremlin.ru/events/president/news/39398.

Menon, K.P.S. (1973), "Indo-Soviet Treaty: Setting and Sequel", New Delhi: Vikas Publishing House Ltd.

MEA (2009), "Annual Report, 2008-2009", New Delhi: Policy Planning and Research Division, Ministry of External Affairs, available at: http://mea.gov.in/Uploads/PublicationDocs/170_Annual-Report-

2008-2009.pdf.

MEA (2010), "Annual Report, 2009-2010", New Delhi: Policy Planning and Research Division, Ministry of External Affairs, available at: http://mea.gov.in/Uploads/PublicationDocs/171_Annual-Report-2009-2010.pdf.

MEA (2015), "Annual Report, 2014-2015", New Delhi: Ministry of external Affairs, available at: http://mea.gov.in/Uploads/PublicationDocs/25009_External_Affairs_2014-2015__English_.pdf.

MEA (2014), "'Druzhba-Dosti: A Vision for Strengthening the Indian-Russian Partnership Over the Next Decade", Joint Statement during the visit of President of the Russian Federation to India", December 11, 2014, available at: http://mea.gov.in/bilateral-documents.htm?dtl/24486/DruzhbaDosti_A_Vision_for_strengthening_the_IndianRussian_Partnership_over_the_next_decade__Joint_Statement_during_the_visit_of_President_of_the_Russia.

Modi, Narendra (2014), "Twitter Message", December 11, 2014, 5. 34 am, available at: https://twitter.com/narendramodi/status/543035981226463234.

Mohanty, Arun (2014), "Fifteenth Indo-Russian Summit", published papers, Eurasian Foundation, available at: http://www.eurasianfoundation.org/index.php/publications/10publications/published-papers.

Nadkarni, Vidya (2010), "Strategic Partnerships in Asia: Balancing without Alliances", Oxon: Routledge.

Naik, J.A. (1995), "Russia's Policy towards India: From Stalin to Yeltsin", New Delhi, M.D. Publications Pvt. Ltd.

Nayar, Baldev Raj and T.V. Paul (2003), "India in the World Order: Searching for Major Power Status", Cambridge: Cambridge University Press.

News Nation Bureau (2014), "Putin: Leader of a Great Nation; India-Russia has a Friendship of Unmatched Mutual Confidence: PM Modi", December 11, 2014, available at: http://www.newsnation.in/article/63519-putin-leader-a-great-nation-india-russia-share-unmatched-mutual-confidence-pm-mo.html.

Press Information Bureau, Government of India, Prime Minister's Office (2014a), "PM meets Russian President Vladimir Putin in

Fortaleza", July 16, 2014, available at: http://www.pib.nic.in/NEWSITE/PrintRelease.aspx?relid=106713.

Press Information Bureau, Government of India, Prime Minister's Office (2014b), "Druzhba-Dosti: A Vision for Strengthening the Indian-Russian Partnership over the Next Decade", Joint Statement during the Visit of President of the Russian Federation to India", December 11, 2014, available at: http://pib.nic.in/newsite/PrintRelease.aspx?relid=113166.

Putin, Vladimir (2000), "Interview with the Indian Media and the Russian RTR TV Channel", October 1, 2000, available at: http://eng.kremlin.ru/transcripts/8737.

Russia and India Report (2015), "Russia, India to Join Hands in Space Monitoring", March 17, 2015, available at: http://in.rbth.com/economics/2015/03/17/russia_india_to_join_hands_in_space_monitoring_42017.html.

Singh, Manmohan (2010), "Speech at 11th India-Russia Annual Summit in 2010", available at: http://rusembindia.com/index.php/component/content/article?id=2119.

Subrahmanyam, K. (1987), "Eradicate the Nuclear Cult", *Bulletin of the Atomic Scientists*, Vol. 4, No. 5, March, pp. 36-39.

Upadhay, Dadan (2014), "Putin-Modi Summit to "Revitalize" Indo-Russian Relations: Indian Ambassador", Russia and India Report, December 5, 2014, available at: http://in.rbth.com/economics/2014/12/05/putin-modi_summit_to_revitalize_indo-russian_relations_-_indian_amb_40181.html.

Vajpayee, A.B. (2000), "Prime Minister of India, Address in Parliament of India", available at: http://parliamentofindia.nic.in/jpi/December2000/CHAP-1.htm.

Zakaria, Fareed (2014), "Interview Transcript: Prime Minister Narendra Modi in a Global Television Exclusive on CNN's Fareed Zakaria GPS", September 22, 2014, available at: http://www.mea.gov.in/Images/pdf/P_M_Narendara_Modi_Interview_Transcript_Eng.pdf.

8

Global Debate on Climate Change and India

Pushpinder Kaur

Origin of Debate

The origin of concerns for environment can be traced back to the 1960s when the paradigm breaking book of Rachel Carson titled *Silent Spring* (1962) and an article of Garrett Hardin's *The Tragedy of the Commons* (1968) set the ball rolling. Consequently, by the end of 1960s, the voice of environmental concern was heard almost uniquely in the West, notwithstanding the damage of the environment in the name of development continued unabated in the communist world, whereas in the developing societies, environmental concerns were regarded as Western luxuries.

The debate got crystallized at United Nations Conference on the Human Environment, held at Stockholm in 1972 and progressed through the subsequent conferences including first world climate change conference in 1979 which articulated that anthropogenic carbon dioxide emissions could have long-term effect on climate. It was followed by the establishment of World Climate Programme (WCP) in 1980 to ensure international cooperation in research regarding climate change and thrashing out the important climate issues of 1980s and 1990s, including ozone depletion and global warming. The World Conservation Strategy (WCT) had further attempted to redefine environmentalism in post-Stockholm period. The World Commission on Environment and Development (WCED) popularly known as Brundtland Commission in its report titled *Our Common Future* submitted in 1987 further spelled out that environment and development are interdependent.

However, the issue was formally articulated at the global

level in 1988, when the United Nations General Assembly (UNGA) passed a resolution recognizing climate change to be a 'common concern of mankind' and urged governments to treat it as a 'priority issue' (UNGA, 1988). It was followed by another resolution passed in 1989 in which the UNGA called on member states to urgently prepare a 'framework convention' to address this global issue through international collaboration (UNGA, 1989). In 1989, the Intergovernmental Panel on Climate Change (IPCC) was established with three working groups focused on the scientific assessment of climate change, environmental and socio-economic impacts, response strategies, foretelling the wide range of challenges that humanity would face as it entered the last decade of the twentieth century. The IPCC has contributed immensely to public understanding of the dangers of global warming particularly in industrialized countries. The First Assessment Report (1990) of IPCC confirmed that the anthropogenic GHG emissions were on rise, and that stabilizing their concentrations in the atmosphere would require 'immediate reduction...of over 60 percent (IPCC, 1990, p. xi).

Further, the UNGA established a negotiating body called the Intergovernmental Negotiating Committee (INC), and directed it to launch formal negotiations to develop an 'effective framework convention on climate change, containing appropriate commitments' (UNGA, 1990). The pressures for action came to a head at the Second World Climate Conference held in Geneva in November 1990, when the Rio Earth Summit was in preparation (Desai, 2012: 374). After intense negotiations in the INC, countries adopted and signed the United Framework Convention on Climate Change (UNFCCC) at the Rio Earth Summit in June 1992. The UNFCCC laid out the basic international political, legal and normative architecture to address climate change (Sengupta, 2012: 102). The core principle agreed under it noted that countries should protect the climate system on the 'basis of equity' and in accordance with their 'common but differentiated responsibilities and respective capabilities' (UNFCCC, 1992, Article 3.1).

United Framework Convention on Climate Change (UNFCCC)

The UNFCCC entered into force in March 1994 and its first Conference of Parties (COP-1) was held in Berlin in 1995, which reviewed the 'adequacy' of the above commitment made by the developed countries (Ibid.). During the negotiations, the developing countries demanded developed countries to act first by talking stringent emission reduction targets by adopting a legally binding protocol to the UNFCCC—as the Montreal Protocol to the Vienna Convention had previously done to combat ozone layer depletion but that was resisted by a group of developed countries including the United States (Oberthur and Ottm, 1999). However, the European Union also favoured the development of protocol, a decision called the '*Berlin Mandate*' which was finally adopted at the end of COP-1, which called for formal negotiations to develop a protocol with legally binding 'targets and time-tables' to reduce industrialized countries' emissions (UNFCCC, 1995). The IPCC's Second Report was released in 1995 which noted a 'discernible human influence' on the global climate (IPCC, 1995: 5) and gave further impetus to this process.

After detailed deliberations, the Kyoto Protocol to the UNFCCC was formally adopted at the COP-3 in December 1997 in which the industrial countries accepted binding obligations on emission reduction by 2008-2012 and that also brought the developing countries indirectly into the mitigation efforts through the Clean Development Mechanism, popularly known as CDM (Desai, 2012: 375). The rules for implementing the Kyoto Protocol were finally adopted at COP-7 of the UNFCCC in 2001 in the form of Marrakesh Accord and the Protocol finally came into force in 2005. The UNFCCC and Kyoto Protocol adopted the 'top-down' approach based on the principle of CBDR. The then largest emitter of GHGs, the US did not implement Kyoto Protocol—as its Congress did not ratify it. Instead, the US advocated a radically altered regime that would replace Kyoto with a less legalized, 'bottom-up', 'pledge and review' type system that would also require significant mitigation commitments and accountability from the key developing countries (Sengupta, 2012: 104).

Keeping in view the end of Kyoto, a period of fresh round of negotiations was set in motion for the second commitment period beyond 2012. However, by this time, the geopolitics of climate diplomacy had changed considerably—as the material reality changed substantially due to the quantum jump in the emission levels of the developing countries in general and China and India in particular. It was argued that the target of temperature increase cannot be arrested unless large emerging economies join in the mitigation effort. According to Sha Zukang, Secretary General of the Rio+20 Conference (2012), "sustainable development is not an option. It is the only path that allows all of humanity to share a decent life on this one planet. Rio+20 give our generation the opportunity to choose this path". The COP-18 in 2012 recommended the second commitment period up to 2020 (Doha Agreement), which imposed a second round of binding commitment of reduction targets of emission of GHGs on 37 countries—with a purpose to ensure emission pathway in the pre-2020 phase before the Paris Agreement would be concluded and come into force.

However, it could not become a reality because only 23 countries—none of the developed countries—had ratified the Agreement whereas, a total of 144 ratifications were required for it to enter into force. In effect, developed countries' rejection of the Kyoto Protocol meant that the differentiated firewall between developed and developing countries was slowly being knocked down and the concept of equity was being given the go by, thereby eroding the fundamental principles of the UNFCCC. Indeed, some new phraseology that is not in the UNFCCC text found its way in the deliberations and decisions of the subsequent Conference of Parties. Finally at the COP-20, that phraseology did not become the part of deliberations but also found place in the final document adopted at the conclusion of conference at Lima in December 2014. It was considered as an attempt by the developed countries' to dilute the ethical principles that form the cornerstones of the convention.

India's Response to Climate Change

The paradox on climate change is that the developed nations account for substantive GHG emissions but the developing countries are paying the price for it. The fallout of climate change may be more severe for developing countries including India—as a majority of their population is still dependent on agriculture for their livelihood. It is argued that due to climate change, India will get more rains when it is not required hence leading to floods and scanty rains in the rainy season leading to droughts that would adversely affect the cropping pattern apart from water borne diseases thereby affecting food security and human survival respectively.

Keeping this in mind, India has already articulated its response to climate change both at the international and national level—as it is an issue that transcends national boundaries. However, the world puts India as the third largest polluting country, but in terms of volume and percentage India's share is a mere 6 percent of the global emissions as compared to China's 29 and USA's 15 percent (Prasad, 2015: 12). When adjusted with population, an average Indian emits four times less than an average Chinese and ten times less than an average American because hundreds of millions of Indians do not have access to electricity. This disparity in the emissions of GHGs has dominated India's position on climate change debate for the last four decades.

Being aware of this fact that climate change is the outcome of the industrialization and consumption patterns of developed nations, New Delhi is also mindful of this fact that ongoing industrialization of developing nations and their increasing population growth are further compounding the problem by increasing their share of carbon emissions. India has realized that the problem of climate change is global in nature having ramifications at the national level, hence needs to be tackled at both the levels.

The 20th session of COPs of the UNFCCC held at Lima in December 2014, mainly had a two-point agenda: to come up with a blue-print for a hopeful Paris Agreement in 2015 and finalize the form and content of Intended Nationally Determined Contributions to be submitted by early 2015 (Sharma, 2014: 9). In other words, on how much each country, rich or poor, is willing to reduce carbon emissions—which were agreed to at the Warsaw talks in 2013. Both aspects remained undecided (Ibid). However, Prodipto Ghosh, who has been a part of several negotiations as the environment secretary and a member of the Prime Minister's Council on Climate Change, (PMCCC) remains hopeful about the world's attention. According to him, at Lima, all countries agreed that they would reveal their goals and plans for greenhouse mitigation to the UN by March 31, 2015. These will not be subjected to any outside review and would be considered in the Paris negotiations, when hopefully some kind of international outcome on climate change in the post-2020 period would emerge (Ibid).

After the Kyoto Protocol's legally binding commitment of the developed countries to reduce (though by very small amount of 5-8 percent) their emissions in a time bound manner, the Lima text now accepts INDCs. The INDCs will also be for all the countries in contrast to the Kyoto Protocol that wanted rich countries to do the mitigation responsible for more emissions. These views may be conflicting, but climate change remains the centrepiece of debate. The IPCC Fifth Assessment Report has warned of catastrophic impacts if decisive actions to limit global warming below 2 degree Celsius are not taken quickly (IPCC, 2015).

In 1992, the developed countries contributed 70 percent of the emissions and by 2014 they were down to 40 percent. The space is filled and now there is little left for the future growth of all. This is where the climate change negotiations are struck. The old rich want the differentiation between the past polluters and the current and the future ones to go. They want to divide the carbon cake afresh. They remind the developing countries that the present is different—China for instance has overtaken the US as the world's largest contributor on an annual basis. But they forget conveniently, that on per capita basis, there is still a vast difference between the US and China, as Soumya Dutta says (Dutta cited in Sharma, 2014: 9).

Notwithstanding this changing scenario, it is argued by the developing countries that today's problems are not because of current emissions rather they are because of what happened in the past. Dealing with climate change requires a complete re-orientation of a country's economy while imposing the emission cut but the developing countries cannot do that till they develop their economies to a certain level. In order to do that also, the developing countries need financial and technological help from the developed world. Most of the time the developmental priorities over rule the environmental concerns in the developing and emerging economies. As stated by Chandrashekhar Dasgupta, a member of Prime Minister Narendra Modi's Council on Climate Change, "India's climate change policy must be based on its national compulsions and not the exigencies of international negotiations. We can and should adopt measures to curb emissions wherever this is possible without slowing down inclusive development" (Dasgupta, 2015: 9).

Over the years, India has built its international stance on fighting climate while keeping in mind the domestic obligations of development enshrined in the CBDR principle. Its proactive submissions to the UN on various issues are in line with the Kyoto Protocol—that India is a developing country, will only do adaptation and to expect mitigation targets is not correct (Ibid). India's principal objective in the entire post-UNFCCC negotiations on climate change from Rio right up to Lima has been to defend this 'differentiated' architecture of the climate regime that it had worked to inscribe within the international law, and to ensure that no fresh legal obligations are placed on it (Sengupta, 2012: 107).

Moving Beyond CBDR Principle

However, the Bali Action Plan requires developing countries to formulate and implement 'Nationally Appropriate Mitigation Actions' (NAMAs), supported and enabled by finance, technology, and capacity building, that are 'monitorable, verifiable and reportable' (MRV). According to India, 'nationally appropriate' signifies that the plans must be prepared by the countries themselves, without external pressure or adjustment and the financial support for NAMAs, or adaptation action plans of developing countries is not an aid but a discharge of responsibility by the developed countries, scaled both by their historical responsibilities for climate change, and the capabilities they have acquired thereby (Ghosh, 2012: 166). Drawing on the fact that India's total emissions had grown by 97 percent between 1990 and 2004, which was noted to be 'one of the highest rates of increase in the world' (UNDP, 2007: 152); and that China has already surpassed the US as the world's largest aggregate emitter of GHGs, a large number of developed countries forcefully argued that no long-term solution to climate change could be found without the active participation of these fast-growing developing states (Sengupta, 2012: 109).

Change in India's Approach from Per Capita Convergence to Per Capita Plus

The first signs of change in India's foreign policy on climate change were seen in July 2009, when Prime Minister, Manmohan Singh signed the Major Economies Forum (MEF) leaders Declaration on Energy and Climate at a meeting held alongside the G-8 Summit in L'Aquila, Italy. The declaration specifically recognized, for the first time, that the rise in global temperature could not exceed 2 degree Celsius, and that MEF countries would work together to identify a 'global goal' to reduce 'global emissions by 2050' (MEF, 2009). While only a political declaration, and not legally binding, India's signing on to this '2 degree Celsius' limit nevertheless signalled its willingness to concede—in theory at least—an implicit cap on its future emissions, even though this was left ambiguous and unstated (Ramachandran, 2015: 5). At Copenhagen, in 2009, India announced to cut its carbon dioxide emitted for each unit of GDP by between 20 and 25 percent by 2020 compared with a baseline of 2005.

Jairam Ramesh, the then Minister for Environment and Forests, Government of India, actively attempted to reframe India's traditional position on this issue few months before the Copenhagen Summit. He argued that it was now in the country's own interest to go beyond its original 'per capita convergence' position and adopt a more aggressive 'per capita plus' approach, whereby specific 'performance targets' could be assigned through domestic legislation or executive action to key sectors of the country's economy—energy, transportation, industry etc. to help to reduce their emissions (Ramesh, 2009).

At the national level, Narendra Modi government has already taken two significant steps. First, he has streamlined energy decision-making, and also environmental decision-making. India's Ministry of Environment and Forests is now the Ministry of Environment, Forests and Climate Change. Second, he has put the experienced and effective Suresh Prabhu as the head of a high level panel on reorganizing the various energy ministries—an "Advisory Group for Integrated Development of Power, Coal and Renewable Energy". The consolidated energy ministries offer the promise of an integrated approach to clean energy (Antholis, 2014: 3).

According to the IPCC Fifth Assessment Report (2014), national governments play key roles in adaptation, planning and implementation through coordinating actions and providing frameworks and support. Institutional dimensions of adaptation governance, including integration of adaptation into planning and decision-making, play a key role in promoting the transition from planning to implementation of adaptation.

Institutional approaches to adaptation involving multiple actors including economic options e.g. insurance, public-private partnership, law and regulations, land zoning laws, national and government policies and programs.

India's National Action Plan on Climate Change (NAPCC) was launched on June 30, 2008 to synergize its developmental needs with sustainability of environment. The first NAPCC outlined existing and future policies and programs addressing climate mitigation and adaptation. It has identified eight "national missions" running through 2017 and instructed the ministries to submit detailed implementation plans to the Prime Minister's Council on Climate Change (PMCCC). The ministries with lead responsibility for each of the missions were directed to develop objective implementation strategies, time lines, and monitoring and evaluation criteria to be submitted to the PMCCC.

Prakash Javadekar, former Minister for Forests, Environment, and Climate Change, acknowledged the legitimacy of environmental concerns, but underscored the need to support big-ticket growth projects in industry and infrastructure, and "fast-track" clearances, without elaborating its operational implications. The developments in the last few months perhaps hold an indication. Forest clearances norms have been diluted. The new National Board for Wildlife has inadequate representation of experts and independent scientists. The National Green Tribunal, India's pioneering and primary entity for dealing with environmental cases, is being reconsidered, jeopardizing a crucial legal avenue for environmental grievances. Perhaps most worryingly, the government is now reviewing existing conservation laws to rewrite them for "current requirements". These are worrying trends for a time when India should be planning for long-term sustainability in the growth agenda, improve transparency in environmental governance, and increase protection for wildlife and biodiversity. Instead, we are dismantling existing frameworks of conservation (Krishnadas and Karnad, 2014: 9).

The Centre for Science and Environment's data (2013)

shows that over 7,00,000 hectares of forest have been cleared for coal and minerals in the last decade alone. These statistics are often glossed over by the development pundits who cry foul over the need for forests and environmental clearances (Ibid). As the environmental laws are side-stepped with shocking disdain, one is forced to reckon with questions of the long-term needs of a larger populace that relies on water, soil, and climate services provided by forests, and the massive losses of habitat and biodiversity that comprises our natural heritage (Ibid).

The real issue is not that of environmental evaluations being an impediment but of enhancing procedural clarity. The Supreme Court, identifying this problem via the Lafarge judgment, asked the Ministry of Environment and Forests to streamline the procedures. The goal was to set simpler and clearer guidelines for applicants, and establish independent authorities for objective assessment and monitoring to ensure compliance with environmental standards, and protect threatened wildlife and their natural habitats. It has not been done yet (Ibid). The Supreme Court of India had stayed all clearances passed by the controversial NBWL, and asked the MoEF to reconstitute the body. The government was forced to adhere to the law. These developments underscore that frameworks for conservation exist in India. It is the question of implementation and improvement (Ibid).

However, the government has now circumvented legal requirements by filling the NBWL ranks with the required number, but a grossly inadequate geographic and the disciplinary representation of experts. The Board is largely constituted of retired bureaucrats, with few experts who have demarcated track record of academics or field excellence in conservation, and with a limited history of engagement with many of our pressing conservation issues, thus curtailing the dissent. The former Environmental Minister Prakash Javadekar used the language of the principle of CBDR at global level—still a relevant concept when India's level of development and per capita emissions are well below the United States or Europe. Yet how those responsibilities are taken within India remains an issue of both Indian and global importance (Antholis, 2014: 4). However, the million dollar question is how to maintain its position based on the principle of CBDR at global negotiations level when the material reality regarding increase of its GHG emissions, has changed substantially over the period of time.

Regarding the reconciling economic development with climate change in India, there are two schools of thought. First argues that the climate change being a burden of history should not be disadvantaged to us when we have given our shot at glory. India should go ahead with its development agenda without caring much about the environmental issues and climate change. The second school of thought articulates that India has to factor climate change seriously while ensuring its economic growth. If India will ignore the environmental concerns in its development strategy then it tends to lose much more in the long-run by entrenching itself in a here-and-now mentality that neglects future costs. New Delhi is required to consider alternatives to the classic growth-at-all-costs paradigm.

Conclusion

To sum up, it can be articulated that the global debate on climate change has travelled a long journey from Stockholm (1972) to Lima (2014) and beyond. During this long journey, it has crossed various milestones ranging from non-binding Stockholm Declaration to the first legally binding treaty, the UNFCCC that was followed by the Kyoto Protocol to implement it. Bring the principle of CBDR principle in its text, the UNFCCC has tried to ensure equity in the climate change legislation apart from addressing the genuine aspirations of developing countries to grow economically without meeting the required climate standards—as it was the necessity to address poverty in developing societies that were lagging behind the developed societies on the ladder of economic development.

Further, the principle of CBDR was considered essential to address the issue of climate change because the poor countries were not responsible for the global warming as per the data with regard to the emission of GHGs in the past is concerned. Due to that, the Kyoto Protocol did not impose any legally binding target regarding the emission cut for the developing countries during the period of first level of commitment from 2008-2012. Although, the largest emitter of GHGs in the atmosphere did not ratify the Kyoto Protocol but the European Union countries have performed reasonably while reducing their GHGs emissions in atmosphere.

The second level of commitment that was expected to start in 2012 and would end in 2020 could not start as the international community has failed to conclude the legally binding agreement for this period. International community did not conclude any treaty as the north-south was sharply divided on the issue of addressing climate change because the north has failed to transfer technology and financial support to poor south countries on the one hand and the developing countries had witnessed the quantum jump in their GHGs emissions on the other. The north countries argued that their action with regard to the reduction of GHGs will be meaningless until and unless the countries from global south act on this count, particularly China, India, Brazil and South Africa. However, the developing countries argued that for the global warming at present, the GHGs emitted by the developed countries in the past are responsible. They further argued that the developing countries cannot reduce the GHG emissions because the developed countries have failed to transfer technology and funds as per the treaty of UNFCCC and Kyoto Protocol.

The negotiations to sign legally binding agreement to reduce the emission of GHGs for the third commitment period that will start from 2020 onward are in progress. However, the recently concluded COP-20 at Lima in December 2014 has once again clearly reflected the north-south divide on this issue but finally they agreed to finalize a more inclusive draft by including both the CBDR and INDCs for the COP-21 held in December 2015 at Paris. Since the last couple of years, the climate change debate has been witnessing a change from the principle of CBDR to INDCs and from the strategy of top-down to bottom-up pledge and review because the material reality has changed substantially as China has replaced US as the largest emitter of GHGs in the atmosphere.

Hence, it is argued that the idea of CBDR has outlived its utility; therefore, the developed world wants the principle of differentiation to go. But the developing countries' argument for the CBDR principle still holds water on two grounds: first, the per capita emission of GHGs in the developing countries is far less that the same in the developed world; second, the developed countries have to transfer technology and funds to reduce the emission of GHGs of developing countries in atmosphere. That is why the draft text of agreement agreed at Lima in December brought back the principle of CBDR on the agenda of treaty to be concluded in COP-21 at Paris in December 2015.

India's position on the issue has been changing along with discourse on climate change. New Delhi was responsible for changing the discourse on climate change in favour of the developing countries when the developed world was shifting the responsibility for global warming on the former. India argued on the behalf of the developing countries while articulating that the poor countries are at the lowest ladder of development and global warming is the product of the emission of GHGs by the developed world during the course of their industrialization apart from their high level of consumption patterns and consumer culture. Therefore, the developed world cannot hold the developing world responsible for historical burden of emission of GHGs. It is the developed world that is responsible. Due to the leading role of India, the discourse on climate change remained favourable to developing societies, despite the consistent efforts by the developed societies to shift responsibilities on the former and finally their concerns including equity, transfer of technology and funds were included in the UNFCCC.

However, the UNFCCC was the first binding international treaty regarding the reduction of emission of GHGs but many developed countries including the United States refused to implement it because the American Congress refused to ratify the Kyoto Protocol to give effect to the UNFCCC. Besides this, the consistent efforts have been on initially to dilute and finally to eliminate the principle of CBDR at the various COPs ranging from COP-1 that happened at Berlin in 1995 to COP-20 that concluded at Lima in December 2014.

However, India along with other developing countries, succeeded to bring the principle of equity, CBDR, transfer of technology and funds back in the Lima text but the developed countries have succeeded to bring the principle of INDCs on the agenda of climate change negotiations. However, New Delhi's position on the issue has been changing since 2009 in the light of changing material reality as it is prepared to move beyond per capita convergence and from top-down to bottom-up approach. It has already taken various steps regarding mitigation and adaptation at home and the National Action Plan on Climate Change is a classic case in point. Much will depend upon the COP-21 held at Paris in 2015 to finalize the biding legal agreement regarding the GHG emission reduction beyond 2020. At the end, it can be articulated that the change in the material reality regarding the emission of GHGs in atmosphere resulted in a shift in the global discourse that has brought change in India's position on climate change.

References

Brundtland Report, "Our Common Future", available at: www.un-document.net/our-common-future.pdf.

Clarke, R. and L. Timberlake (1982), "Stockholm Plus Ten-Promises, Promises? The Decade since the 1972 UN Environment Conference", London, Earthscan.

Carson, Rachel (1962), "Silent Spring", New York: Houghton Mifflin.

Dasgupta, Chandrashekhar (2015), "India and Climate Change: Need for Updated Plan", *The Tribune*, January 20.

Desai, Nitin (2012), "The Geopolitics of Climate Change", in Navroz K. Dubash (ed.), 'Handbook on Climate Change and India: Development, Politics and Governance', New Delhi: Oxford University Press, pp. 373-384.

Ghosh, Prodipto (2012), "Climate Change Debate: The Rationale of India's Position", in Navroz K. Dubash (ed.), 'Handbook on Climate Change and India: Development, Politics and Governance', New Delhi: Oxford University Press, pp. 157-169.

Hardin, Garrett (1968), "The Tragedy of the Commons", *Science,* 162, pp. 1243-1248.

IPCC (1990), "The First IPCC Assessment Reports", Intergovernmental Panel on Climate Change, Geneva Switzerland.

IPCC (1995), "The Second IPCC Assessment Reports", Intergovernmental Panel on Climate Change, Geneva, Switzerland.

IPCC (2015), "The Fifth IPCC Assessment Reports", Intergovernmental Panel on Climate Change, Geneva, Switzerland.

Khor, Martin (2015), "Understanding the Lima Climate Conference: A Proxy Battle for the 2015 Paris Agreement", *Economic and Political Weekly*, Vol. 1, No. 6, February 7, pp. 37-44.

Krishnadas, Meghna and D. Karnad (2014) "Green Rules: Old Debates, New Dialogue", *The Tribune*, October 3.

Long, B.L. (2000), "International Environmental Issues and the OECD, 1950-2000: An Historical Perspective", Paris, Organization for Economic Cooperation and Development.

"National Action Plan on Climate Change", Government of India. New Delhi, June 30, 2008.

Oberthur, S. and H.E. Ottm (1999), "The Kyoto Protocol: International Climate Policy for the 21st Century", Berlin: Springer.

"Fifth Assessment Synthesis Report", United Nations, 2014, pp. 1-35.

Prasad, K.V. (2015), "What Obamas' Visit Means for India", *The Tribune*, January 25.

Ramachandran, R. (2015), "More Hot Air", *Frontline*, Vol. 32, No. 1, January 10-23, pp. 104-108.

Ramesh, Jairam (2015), "I Want to Position India as a Proactive Player", *Mint*, September 29, available at: www.livemint.com.

Sharma, Vibha (2014), "Earth Heats up, World Cold to Deal", *The Tribune*, December 21.

Sengupta, Sandeep (2012), "International Climate Negotiations and India's Role", in Navroz K. Dubash (ed.), 'Handbook on Climate Change and India: Development, Politics and Governance', New Delhi: Oxford University Press, pp. 101-117.

UNDP (2007), "Fighting Climate Change: Human Solidarity in a Divided World", Human Development Report, 2007/2008, Basingstoke: Palgrave Macmillan.

UNFCCC (1995), "Berlin Mandate", Decision 1/CP.1 in FCCC/1995/7/Add.1, June 6.

UNFCCC (2007), "Report of the Conference of the Parties 13, held at Bali", December 3-15, available at: unfccc.int/resources/docs/2007/cop13/eng/06a01.pdf.

UNFCCC (2013), "Report of the Conference of the Parties-19, held at Warsaw", November 11-22.

UNFCCC (2014), "Report of the Conference of the Parties-20, held at Lima", December 1-12.

William J. Antholis, "India's Climate Change Policy in a Modi Government", available at: http://www.brookings.edu/blogs/planetpolicy/posts/2014/07/30-India-Climate-Change.

9

Dynamics of Terrorism in India

Shivani Sharma

Introduction

The attacks of September 11 on the US and the war on terrorism launched in the aftermath, opened a paradigm debate on the most principled notion of terrorism. Terrorism is one of the most complex and also the most complicated phenomenon of the contemporary world. Impression of what terrorism is lacks a precise, concrete and truly explanatory definition of the word.

The most generalised definition of terrorism defines it as, illegal violence or threatened violence directed against human or non-human objects, provided that it;

- was undertaken or ordered with a view to altering or maintaining at least one putative norm in at least one particular territorial unit or population.
- had secretive, furtive and clandestine features that were expected by the participants to conceal their personal identity or their future location.
- was not undertaken or ordered to further the permanent defence of some area.
- was not conventional warfare and because of their concealed personal liberty, concealment of their future location, their threats or their spatial mobility, the participants perceived themselves as less vulnerable to conventional military action.
- was perceived by the participants as contributing to the normative goal previously described by inculcating fear of violence in persons other than the immediate target of the actual or threatened violence or publicizing some cause (Gibbs, 2012: 64).

Walter Laqueur, argues that terrorism has appeared in so many different forms and under so many different circumstances that a comprehensive definition of the term is impossible (Weinberg, 2012: 76). Whereas, Alex Schmid after analysing the content of 109 definitions of terrorism, defined it as "an anxiety inspiring method of repeated violent action, employed by (semi-) clandestine individual, group or state actors, for idiosyncratic, criminal or political reasons, whereby, in contrast to assassination, the direct targets of violence are not the main targets. The immediate human victims of violence are generally chosen randomly or selectively from a target population and serve as message generators" (Hoefler, 2012: 84).

While describing the term terrorism, Alex Schimd found that terrorism is an abstract concept with no real essence and that the meaning of terrorism is usually derived from the support to the victim or target. As US Attorney General, Ramsey Clarke once noted, "one man's terrorist is another man's freedom fighter". The ambivalence around the meaning of the term "terrorism" often ignores the fundamental differences between terrorism and the legitimate and regulated uses of violence.

The UN Secretary-General's High level Panel Report, 2004, defined terrorism as: "any action that is intended to cause death or serious bodily harm to civilians or non-combatants, when the purpose of such activities by its nature or context, is to intimidate a population or to compel a government of an international organization to do or abstain from doing any act" (Crenshaw, 2011: 2).

Thus, terrorism as a term lacks a self-sufficient definition and the task of defining it remains highly problematic. The term terrorism dates back to the times of French Revolution. However, the 9/11 attacks waged on the powerful American symbols by the radical groups is said and believed to have marked a "new" wave of terrorism.

Changing Dynamics of Terrorism

After the attacks of September 11, 2001, it was believed

that the world was confronting a "new" form of terrorism. As Bruce Hoffman concluded, "the growth of religious terrorism and its emergence in recent years is a driving force behind the increasing lethality of international terrorism that shatters some of the most basic assumptions about terrorists and the violence they commit" (Hoffman, 1998: 200). Broadly, the new paradigm holds that modern terrorism has different motives, different actors, different sponsors and greater lethality than the traditional terrorism.

Goals

The ends of the new terrorism are presumed to be both unlimited and non-negotiable and are considered largely incomprehensible and amorphous. From the perspective of the new terrorism school of thought, religious doctrines emphasizing on transformational and apocalyptic beliefs are the main drivers and motivators for the new terrorism. Walter Lacquer, for example, characterises the new terrorists as religious fanatics who suffer from delusion and persecution mania (Lacquer, 1999).

However, attributing religion to be the main motivator for terrorism has been questioned because religion is considered to be a problematic label which implies a mono causal explanation that does no justice to rich practice of terrorist activity (Duyvesteyn, 2010: 446). Therefore, new terrorism can be both seen as political and religious. Though, religion has played a role in the formulation of the terrorist targets, they are translated to clear political positions related to clear political targets, such as, the spread of political Islam and the establishment of the Caliphate.

Methods

The means of the new terrorism are also considered to be radically different from the past. The premise is that because the ends of the new terrorism are unlimited, so, too are the means that the groups espousing these goals are willing and able to use.

According to Walter Lacquer, the new terrorism is different in character (from the old), aiming not at clearly defined political demands but at the destruction of society and the elimination of a large series of the population (Lacquer, 1996). Jessica Stern argues that the risk of terrorist use of nuclear, chemical or biological weapons against civilians is growing not just because of the increased availability of such weapons but because of changes in terrorist motivation (Stern, 2003).

Organization and Resources

The organization of the new terrorism is thought to be fundamentally different from earlier structures of terrorist actors. The new terrorists are said to be decentralised, with a flat networked apparatus rather than a hierarchical or cellular structure. New terrorist organizations flatten out their pyramids of authority and control and approach a network form, a group of more or less autonomous, dispersed entities, linked by advanced communications and a common purpose. The proliferation of the amateur terrorists and the ad-hoc terrorist groups come together with the like mindedness to conduct a terrorist attack and disband (Tucker, 2001: 3).

The attacks of September 11 on the US and the war on terrorism launched aftermath, not only marked the start of the first "globalised war" of the 21st century but also challenged the traditional security threats faced by the nation-states rooted in protecting one's borders militarily. This has raised many issues pertaining to "transnational conflict", "violence" and "globalization". The war on terrorism thus, became a war waged against the transnational terrorist groups operating all around the world and the rogue states that are in support of them. The transnational nature of the threat made the war against terrorism a transnational conflict wherein states, not directly involved in the fight became participants to the war in order to combat the large network of terrorist groups operating in different parts of the world.

The rise of transnational terrorist organizations such as the

Al-Qaeda and Taliban changed the landscape of terrorism. Al-Qaeda today, has become more of an idea or a concept than an organization possessing a novel structure, an amorphous movement having a robust capacity for regeneration and a very diverse membership that cuts across ethnic, class, and national boundaries (Gunaratna, 2002: 54). Al-Qaeda as Hoffman describes is pursuing a "war of attrition" against its enemies. The group today is a more diffuse phenomenon, and is a remarkably nimble, flexible and adaptive entity. It has become a transnational movement and a decentralised global network of Islamic extremists which has resulted in many Al-Qaeda's today than just one (Hoffman, 2005: 10).

Thus, the group has become a vast enterprise—an international movement or franchise operation with the like-minded local representatives, loosely connected to a central ideological or motivational base, but advancing their common goal independently of one another (Hoffman, 2010: 552). The group's ideology is profoundly internationalist in its reach based on "Islamism" and "global jihad", describing Jihad as a religious obligation and duty of every Muslim in defence of Islam and Muslims against a defined enemy (Herd, 2007). Thus, the global reach of the group attempts to contextualise local conflicts as part of a broader global struggle against "apostasy" and the "infidel" (Rabasa, 2006: 9). Drawing from the above, the next section will deal with the threats that the Indian state faces from the transnational terrorist organizations, aided and supported by some of the states and the foreign terrorist organizations.

Challenges to India's Security

Terrorism is the most challenging security threat that India is dealing with. India has long been the victim of cross-border terrorism and proxy violence emanating from the soils of its immediate neighbour, Pakistan. According to the National Consortium for the Study of Terrorism and Responses to Terrorism (START), approximately 400 people were killed as a result of terrorist attacks in India in 2013. [1] India, thus, remains subject to violent terrorist attacks and continues to be one of the most persistently targeted countries by transnational and domestic terrorist groups.

The genesis of the present day insurgency and terrorism in the state of Jammu and Kashmir has its roots back in the history of partition. India and Pakistan look at terrorism from two diametrically opposite ends, one as, Kashmir related separatism as terrorism backed by Pakistan and the other from a prism of an illegal occupation of Kashmir by foreign forces respectively. Terrorism, thus, has become essentially a nationalistic conflict, morphed into a religious war with global implications (Weaver, 2002).

The growing spread of militancy and terrorism in South Asia can be traced back to the Afghan war of the 1980s. The Soviet occupation of Afghanistan involved the South Asian region in the Cold War politics and dragged other regional players like Pakistan into the conflict. Being a "frontline" state to the US and under the military rule of Zia-Ul-Haq, Pakistan extended unstinting support to the Islamic groups by providing massive arms and economic support to the Mujahideen forces to oust the Soviets from Afghanistan. As a consequence of the joint collaboration between the Pakistani army and the American CIA, the then "freedom fighters" were transformed into Mujahideen forces and were used to counter India on the Kashmir front (Abbas, 2006). Therefore, in the process of rendering support to the Afghan militancy, Pakistan itself went through a process of radicalisation. At the end of the war, the Afghan refugees trained by the Pakistani establishment were later used as proxies to support the militancy in Kashmir. Groups such as Jaish-e-Mohammad (JeM), Harkat-ul-Mujahideen and Lashkar-e-Taiba (LeT) which have traditionally focussed on Kashmir, became a vital component of Islamabad's regional strategy.

While knowing about India's conventional power superiority, Pakistan formally adopted the policy of proxies, to "bleed India through thousand cuts" by engaging it in a low-intensity conflict in Kashmir. Proxies for Pakistan, therefore, proved to be a low cost and until recently, a relatively low risk method to tie down a disproportionate number of Indian troops and to make sure that the Kashmir issue remains in spotlight. Moreover, by ensuring that the Indian portion of Kashmir remains an insurgency, Pakistan and its proxies have also frustrated Indian efforts to fully incorporate Kashmir into the country (Clarke, 2010: 34). The state of Pakistan, especially the army and the intelligence wing, has supported the functioning of most radical Islamic groups on a wider stage, equipping and training them when necessary and providing overall political and strategic guidance to them. Armed with sophisticated weapons, motivated through religious indoctrination and convinced about their dedication to the new kind of Islam, the new breed of Islamic jihadis emerged as a new tool to execute the foreign policy objectives of Pakistan (Pattnaik, 2002: 202).

On the other hand, Pakistan has a long history of religious radicalism and extremism where militant groups and organizations operating within Pakistan enjoy relative impunity and immunity from the state apparatus. The state has been providing unstinted support to the radical groups considering the Kashmiri based militants as "freedom fighters" or "Mujahideens" that are fighting for a just cause in their effort to free Kashmiri people from the perceived Indian oppression. However, these organizations often strive for different political and religious objectives and sectarian affiliations. Therefore, in order to understand Pakistan's policy towards terrorism and militancy, it is imperative to broadly classify and categorise the various existing militant organizations operating within Pakistan:

- Groups that have traditionally focussed on Kashmir. This category includes Deobandi organizations such as Jaish-e-Mohammad (JeM), Harkat-ul-Mujahideen (HUM); Ahle Hadith organizations such as Lashkar-e-Taiba (LeT); and those groups under the influence of the Jamaat-e-Islami

(JI) such as Al-Badr and Hizbul Mujahideen (HM).

- Groups that have traditionally been sectarian in nature. These include the anti-shia's Lashkar-e-Jhangvi (LeJ) and Sipah-e-Sahaba Pakistan.
- Anti state militant groups. Most prominent is the Muttahida Quami Movement (MQM) and its breakaway organizations such as TTP, which perpetrate violence against the state in pursuit of their political objectives (Fair, 2009: 85).

Pakistan's policy of "selective" counter-terrorism, fighting only an arm of the Jihadist Frankenstein while tolerating the other section of radicals has made Pakistan a victim of terrorism itself. The narrative of "good" and "bad" terrorism and the official discriminating response towards the radical groups has made Pakistan a hotbed of militancy and terrorism. It was under Musharraf's rule that Pakistan distinguished between "good" and "bad" Taliban: those with ties to the ISI enjoyed protection, whereas the ones trying to operate independently or attacking Pakistan's security forces were targeted for elimination (Haqqani, 2013: 327). Pakistan thus, was warehousing some extremists and leaving others untouched.

Whereas, in the wake of 9/11 attacks, the transnational terrorist groups such as the Al-Qaeda and Taliban found sanctuaries and refugee in the Pakistan's Federally Administered Tribal Areas (FATA). Thus, the militants in the FATA and the North West Frontier Province painted their struggle in Islamic terms, which resulted in the formation of many new militant groups within Pakistan and the existing ones siding with the ongoing Al-Qaeda's war against the enemies of Islam (Rashid, 2010). While employing the rhetoric of religion in justifying their militant activities, and professing it to be a duty of all Muslims to wage jihad against the non-believers, the foreign militants influenced the indigenous groups to justify their actions in the name of religion. On the other hand, Al-Qaeda and its members closely networked with the militant groups operating within

Pakistan and received personnel and sanctuary support in the tribal areas of the country (Zimmerman, 2013).

Furthermore, terrorism not only serves as a major security threat to India but is also a significant factor dictating the course of foreign policy relations with its neighbour, Pakistan. Indian Prime Minister, Narendra Modi at the UN General Assembly, 2014 noticeably stated, "We want to promote friendship with Pakistan too, but we can only talk without the shadow of terrorism over us". [2] The 2001 Indian Parliament attack and the alleged involvement of Pakistani based groups LeT and JeM paralysed the Indo-Pakistan relations. It was L.K. Advani, the then Home Minister of India who stated, "Terrorism in India is the handiwork of Pakistan based terrorist outfits known to derive their support and sustenance from Pakistan ISI". [3] Former Indian Prime Minister, Atal Bihari Vajpayee at the CICA Summit also proclaimed that although repeated assurances were made by the Pakistan President Musharraf for not letting its territory being used to promote terrorism, cross-border infiltration has increased and violence in Jammu and Kashmir remains unabated. The involvement of Pakistan's intelligence agency, ISI in sponsoring the cross-border terrorism despite Musharaf's pledge to the US and UK on June 6, 2002 to stop cross-border infiltration "permanently" in Kashmir furthered the "trust-deficit" between the two states (Chaudhury, 2003: 28).

However, despite condemning the attacks on the Indian Parliament, Pakistan maintained that it would continue to provide moral, diplomatic, and political support to Kashmiris. Whereas, the Indian state has made it ardently clear that for any talks to follow, cross-border terrorism needs to end from the Pakistani side.

Many efforts were taken by both the sides to proclaim peace between the two states during 2003 to 2007. India and Pakistan signed a formal ceasefire agreement in 2003 along the international border, the Line of Control and the Actual Ground Position Line in Jammu and Kashmir. A major step forward in the peace process was taken on the condition that cross-border terrorism has to stop to allow the ceasefire to hold. Talks on terrorism along with drug smuggling were held at home/interior secretary level.

The first meeting in this regard was held on August 10-11, 2004 in Islamabad. The second round of talks was held on August 30, 2005 during which both sides agreed to jointly fight terrorism and increase co-operation between intelligence agencies (Noor, 2007: 73). However, the bomb blasts in commuter trains in Mumbai on July 11, 2006 posed hurdles in the peace process in which the then Indian Prime Minister, Manmohan Singh asked Pakistan to halt such activities, for it was difficult to carry forward the peace process.

However, the relations reached a new low after the Mumbai-terror attacks of November 26, 2008. Subsequent investigations into the attacks once again established the attackers to be Pakistani nationals, having their links to LeT. The then Indian Prime Minister, Manmohan Singh noted that "the well planned and well orchestrated attacks, probably with external linkages, were intended to create a sense of panic, by choosing high profile targets and indiscriminately killing foreigners".

He further stated, "We will take up strongly with our neighbours that the use of their territory for launching attacks on us will not be tolerated, and that there would be a cost if suitable measures are not taken up by them". [4]

However, despite the lone terrorist being caught alive by the Indian security forces and confessed to being a Pakistani, Pakistan denied the allegations despite having made a statement of condemning the attacks and offering to co-operate in the investigations. The relations further deteriorated when Pakistan refused to put the Mumbai attackers to justice and referred to the evidence provided by India as mere information. Since, no war could be proclaimed against Pakistan as noted by the Indian Defence Minister, A.K. Antony on December 16, 2008, a firm message and warning was sent to Pakistan to act against terrorism if it sought stable relations with India.

Pakistan's commitment to battle the radical elements in the society has always been seen with suspicion by the international community. Washington too has shown distrust towards Pakistan's security apparatus, especially the ISI, because of its alleged support to the Taliban by providing weapons, ammunition, intelligence and even direction to suicide bombings (Jones, 2007). Joseph Dunford, Commander of the US and NATO forces in Afghanistan, noted that the Afghan Taliban and the Haqqani network have sanctuaries inside Pakistan and there are intelligence reports about their links with the ISI. [5] US Military Chief Admiral Mullen calls the Haqqani network as a "veritable arm" of Pakistan's Intelligence Agency. [6] Moreover, the documents made available by Wikileaks suggest that Pakistan, an ostensible ally of the US, allows representatives of its spy service to meet directly with the Taliban in secret strategy sessions to organize networks of militant groups that fight against American soldiers in Afghanistan and even hatch plots to assassinate Afghan leaders. [7]

Zahid Hussain, a distinguished Pakistani journalist, cites evidence of two former ISI Directors, General Hamid Gul and Javed Nasir's involvement in Islamist radical movement linked to the Al-Qaeda and the Taliban (Hussain, 2007). However, the presence of Osama Bin Laden in his fortified compound in Abbotabad, near the Pakistan military station on May 1, 2001, raised many hard questions about Pakistan's commitment to combat terrorism.

Under the US pressure, and in yet another bid to strengthen the legal regime, the Pakistani government issued the "Anti-Terrorist (Amendment) Ordinance" on November 16, 2002. The amendment led to the banning of six terrorist organizations, involving the Kashmir based radical groups, Jaish-e-Muhammad, Lashkar-e-Taiba, and other sectarian radical organizations, Sipah-e-Sahaba (SSP), Tehrik-e-Jafria Pakistan (TJP), Tehrik-e-Nifaze-Shariat-e-Muhammadi and Tehreek-e-Islami. Though, despite the policy actions undertaken by the Pakistani government, the country's record in dealing with such radical groups has been highly duplicitous. The disbanding and banning of such radical organizations have had no impact on the membership, leadership and finances of these operational groups. The banning usually implies a name change or a temporary suspension of operations. For example, Lashkar-e-Taiba under the leadership of Hafiz Saeed was banned and regrouped under a new name of Jammat-ud-Dawa, which claims to be a "humanitarian charity" organization.

Despite, India's repeated accusation to Pakistan for aiding and abetting the insurgency in Kashmir, the Pakistani response has been ambivalent and reiterates its long held position of it extending its "moral, diplomatic and political support to the freedom fighters" in Jammu and Kashmir (Behra, 2001: 304). The support rendered to the radical forces and the Pakistani sponsored cross-border terrorism has become an important issue on which the process of dialogue between India and Pakistan hinges. The meeting of the Pakistan High Commissioner in New Delhi, Abdul Basit with the Kashmiri Hurriyat leaders on August 2014 bore serious implications on India-Pakistan relations, resulting in the suspension of Foreign Secretary level talks between them.

Therefore, terrorism not only poses a major security threat to India but also dominates the course of normalization process with its neighbour Pakistan.

Counter-Terrorism Policy: Challenges and Prospects

This section will dwell upon questions such as: Does India have a counter-terrorism policy? What are the challenges that India faces, and what it can do in terms of its institutional structure, its domestic capabilities, political will and support from international partners to fight terrorism?

India's response to terrorism has been episodic and lacks a comprehensive counter-terrorism strategy and policy. The Indian response to the terrorist activities has been two-fold, political and military. Though, in the wake of nuclearisation, military solutions have become less of an option. Whereas, diplomacy and international co-operation are considered as more viable options since no military operation can have strategic level effects without risking military responses from the other side. Thus, for a changed landscape of terrorism, cloaked with an element of denial, India must adopt a policy that includes eliminating the cause of militancy and resort to international diplomacy to make it expensive for any state to exercise this option against it.

The 2008 Mumbai attacks exposed many of India's enduring vulnerabilities on its national security. The intelligence failure, lack of co-ordination between the central security agencies like RAW and IB and the local police, gaps in coastal surveillance, delay in the arrival of NSG and inadequate counter-terrorism training and equipment for the local police led the Indian government to announce a number of reforms in addressing these shortcomings.

Though, following the attacks on the commuter trains in Mumbai in 2006, India formalised its first counter-insurgency doctrine, "Integrated Defence Staff, 2006" which called for a unity of efforts across India's military, political, paramilitary and intelligence agencies. However, it was only after the Mumbai attacks that the Indian state made efforts to enhance its domestic capabilities to counter terrorism through agencies such as the Central Bureau of Investigation (CBI), National Security Guards (NSG), National Investigative Agency (NIA) and making amendments to the prevailing detention laws. The NIA was empowered to deal with terrorism across states without seeking special permission from the states. The specially trained National Security Guards along with paramilitary forces like the Centre Reserve Police Force, Central Industrial Security Force and the Border Security Forces were deployed to check on the terrorist activities and situations. The Unlawful Prevention Act provided new powers to the security forces, including the ability to hold suspects for six months without charges.

India, thus, has a large and complex bureaucratic set up to manage its counter-terrorism efforts. However, its efforts to counter-terrorism are seriously hampered by impediments to coordination and information sharing between the agencies. In order to address some of the challenges, India launched a Multi-Agency Centre for enhancing intelligence gathering and sharing. Moreover, the Second Administrative Reforms Commission in its report titled "Combating Terrorism" recommended the establishment of National Counter-Terrorism Centre (NCTC) located in the Intelligence Bureau (IB). The main functions were to be as follows:

- To draw up plans and co-ordinate actions for counter-terrorism.
- To integrate intelligence pertaining to terrorism; analyse the same; pursue or mandate other agencies to pursue the different leads; and to coordinate with the existing agencies for an effective response.
- To maintain a comprehensive database of terrorists and their associates.
- To ensure that all agencies have access to and receive source intelligence support that is necessary to execute counter-terrorism plans and accomplish their assigned tasks.
- To coordinate with existing investigation and intelligence agencies to ensure that all terrorist cases are solved and the perpetrators are brought to justice; and
- To prepare daily threat assessment review and disseminate them to the appropriate levels in the Central government and the state governments (Office Memorandum, NCTC order, 2012)). [8]

It also plans to implement the National Intelligence Grid (NATGRID), a system of linking database in different government departments and ministries for use by intelligence agencies.

Since, transnational terrorism cannot be fought alone; India along with making domestic efforts must also engage and participate fully with international actors to fight the global war on terrorism. The very evolution of terrorist organization such as the Al-Qaeda and Taliban into a loose, flexible network with small informal groups, compounds the challenges of combating the spread of terrorism. Therefore, it has become vital to strengthen the international mechanism to tackle the menace of terrorism by marshalling and sustaining international coalitions in order to defeat the global network of terrorists and prevent the growth of new organizations. The United Nations Security Council Resolution 1373 (2001) called upon all member states to cooperate to prevent terrorist attacks through a spectrum of activities, including suppressing and freezing terrorist financing, prohibiting their nationals from financially supporting terrorists, and taking steps to prevent the movement of terrorists. [9]

The resolution reaffirmed the primacy of local efforts in bearing primary responsibility for fighting terrorism within its territory and adopting a zero tolerance policy on terrorist activities within their borders. The General Assembly on September 8, 2006 adopted the UN Global Counter-Terrorism Strategy, which united all 192 member states for the first time, reflecting international community's resolve to combat the scourge of terrorism. [10]

India has been working along the global counter-terrorism strategy and with the international community. While recalling to the commitments of member states with regard to the implementation of General Assembly and Security Council resolutions relating to international terrorism, India must take recourse of the international partners to put adequate pressure on the states aiding and abetting terrorism.

The counter-terrorist strategy requires proactive security cooperation with and support of countries under assault by the Al-Qaeda and its affiliates. Hence, the transnational warfare in the aftermath of the 9/11 attacks bore implications both domestically and globally for the countries. The post-9/11 world order indicates the changed dynamics of world politics, where the issues at home and its responses cut across national boundaries and overcome geographical constraints.

India has been a major player and also a signatory to the United Nations Security Council resolution to tackle terrorism. Moreover, India has also furthered bilateral efforts in countering terrorism as India and the US re-affirmed their commitment to, and the importance of bilateral counter-terrorism cooperation. In May 2013, the second US-India Homeland Security Dialogue took place in Washington and in December India hosted the US-India Homeland Security Dialogue Police chief conference, a landmark event that brought together US and Indian law enforcement officials to share best practices and lessons learnt in detecting, preventing and responding to threats facing large cities, including terrorist threats (Country Response on Terrorism Report, 2013).

At a regional level, India signed a joint declaration with ASEAN to combat international terrorism at Bali, Indonesia on October 8, 2003. [11] The SAARC Regional Convention on Suppression of Terrorism signed by the regional members and other successive moves undertaken was on account to meet the obligations devolving on member states in terms of the Security Council Resolution 1373 and the International Convention for suppression of financing of terrorism.

With the growing threat of terrorism to the national security, India must evolve a national policy on countering terrorism. The long porous borders and coastlines, relatively limited numbers of well trained personnel and inadequate intelligence sharing, compounds the challenges of fighting security threats for the Indian state. Pakistan continues to perceive India as a threat and thereby supports the radical elements against the Indian state. Contrarily, the operation of foreign terrorists all over India and having ties with the indigenous terrorist organizations such as the SIMI and IM makes the surveillance more difficult.

Thus, the Indian state should go beyond a "reactive" policy to combat terrorism and must adopt a pro-active, preventive and pre-emptive strategy to counter the emerging threats. An integrated Homeland Security Strategy has become the need of the hour as India needs to work at multiple scales and dimensions on a long-term basis. Moreover, the events of September 11 have focussed world attention towards countering terrorism in all its manifestations. Therefore, India must also move along the changed dynamics of terrorism to address its own problems of terrorism and evolve a coherent and comprehensive counter-terrorism policy.

Endnotes

1. "US Department of Action: Country Report: South and Central Asia" (2013), available at: http://www.state.gov/j/ct/rls/crt/2013/224824.htm.
2. Narendra Modi speech at the United Nations Security Council, September 27, 2014, available at: http://www.un.org/en/ga/69/meetings/gadebate/27sep/india.shtm.
3. Statement made by L.K. Advani, the then Union Home Minister in Lok Sabha, December 18, 2001.
4. Text of PM Manmohan Singh (2008), available at: http://www.andhranews.net/India/2008/November/27-Text-Prime-Minister-Manmohan-Singh-76232.asp.
5. "ISI Has Links with Haqqani Network", *Deccan Herald*, April 16, 2013, available at: http://www.deccanherald.com/content/326528/isi-has-links-haqqaninetwork.
6. Haqqani network is one of the members of the allied faction that are fighting the US and NATO troops in Afghanistan. It is an Afghan insurgent organization and maintain safe heaven in North Waziristan. It is a useful ally and proxy force to the Pakistan Security Establishment in protecting their interests in Afghanistan.
7. "Pakistan Aids Insurgency in Afghanistan, Reports Assert", *The New York Times,* July 25, 2010, available at: http://www.nytimes.com/2010/07/26/world/asia/26isi.html?_r=0.
8. "National Counter Terrorism Centre Memorandum", South Asia Terrorism Portal (2012), available at: http://www.satp.org/satporgtp/countries/india/document/papers/2012/NCTC_2012.pdf.

9. "United Nations Security Council Resolution 1373", United Nations, September 28, 2001, available at: http://www.un.org/en/sc/ctc/specialmeetings/2012/docs/United%20Nations%20Security%20Council%20Resolution%201373%20(2001).pdf.
10. "Working Group on Radicalisation and Extremism", United Nations (2007), available at: http://www.un.org/en/terrorism/pdfs/radicalization.pdf.
11. ASEAN (2003), "ASEAN-India Joint Declaration for co-operation to combat International Terrorism", available at: http://www.asean.org/news/item/asean-india-joint-declaration-for cooperation-to-combat-international-terrorism-2.

References

Abbas, Hasan (2006), "Pakistan's Drift into Extremism: Allah, the Army and America's War on Terrorism", New York: M.E. Sharp.

Behera, Ajay Darshan (2001), "The Supporting Structure for Pakistan's Proxy War in Jammu and Kashmir", *Strategic Analysis*, 25(3): 393-410.

Bhasin, Avtar Singh (2011), "India-Pakistan Relations, 1947-2007", New Delhi: Public Diplomacy Division, Ministry of External Affairs, Government of India.

Chaudhury, Rahul (2003), "India's Response to Terrorism after December 13, 2001", *Conflict, Security and Development*, 3(2): 277-285.

Clarke, Ryan (2010), "Lashkar-e-Taiba: Roots, Logistics, Partnerships and the Fallacy of Subservient Proxies", *Terrorism and Proxy Violence*, 22(3): 394-417.

Crenshaw, Marth (2011), "Explaining Terrorism: Causes, Processes and Consequences", London: Routledge.

Duyvesteyn, Isabelle (2010), "How New is the New Terrorism", *Studies in Conflict and Terrorism*, 27(5): 439-454.

Fair, Christine and Jacob N. Shaprio (2009), "Understanding support for militancy in Pakistan", *International Security*, 34(3): 79-118.

Gibbs, Jack (2012), "Conceptualisation of Terrorism" in Horgan, John and Kurt Braddock (eds.), 'Terrorism Studies: A Reader', London: Routledge.

Gunaratna, Rohan (2002), "Inside Al-Qaeda: Global Network of Terrorism", New York: Columbia University Press.

Herd, G. (2007), "Approaches to Countering Terrorism and CIST" in Aldis, A. and G.P. Herd (eds.), 'The Ideological War on Terrorism: Worldwide Strategies for Countering Terrorism', London: Routledge.

Hoffman, Bruce (2010), "The Changing Face of Al-Qaeda and the Global War on Terrorism", *Studies in Conflict and Terrorism*, 27(6): 549-560.

Hoffman, Bruce (1998), "Inside Terrorism", London: St. Andrews.

Hussain, Haqqani (2013), "Magnificent Delusions: Pakistan, the United States and an Epic History of Misunderstanding", United States: Public Affairs.

Hussain, Zahid (2007), "Frontline Pakistan: The Struggle with Militant Islam", London: I.B. Tauris.

Lacquer, Walter (1996), "Post Modernist Terrorism", *Foreign Affairs*, 75(5): 24-28.

Lacquer, Walter (1999), "The New Terrorism: Fanatism and Arms of Mass Destruction", New York: Oxford University Press.

Noor, Sanam (2007), "Pakistan-India Relations and Terrorism", *Pakistan Horizon*, 60(2): 65-84.

Pattnaik, Smruti (2002), "Pakistan's Kashmir Policy: Objectives and Approaches", *Strategic Analysis*, 26(2): 199-225.

Rabasa, Angel, et al. (2006), "Beyond Al-Qaeda: The Global Jihadist Movement", US: RAND Corporation.

Rashid, Ahmed (2010), "The Situation in Pakistan", *Asian Affairs*, 41(3): 367-380.

Stern, Jessica (2003), "Terror in the Name of God: Why Religious Militants Kill", Florida: Eproject Band.

Tucker, David (2001), "What's New About New Terrorism and How Dangerous Is It", *Terrorism and Political Violence*, 13(3): 1-14.

Weaver, Mary Anne (2002), "Pakistan: In the Shadow of Jihad and Afghanistan", New York: Faraar, Straus and Giroux.

Weinberg, Leonard (2012), "The challenge of Conceptualising Terrorism", in Horgan, John and Kurt Braddock (eds.), 'Terrorism Studies: A Reader', London: Routledge.

10

Cyber Security in India

Chandrakant Chellany [1]

As nation-states get deeply embedded within cyber space, conventional wisdom on politics and strategy runs into crisis. While various actors—from individuals to nations—appear keen to benefit from the opportunities afforded by cyber space, they also remain uncertain about its long-term effects. Policymakers are usually found trailing behind this hyper dynamic phenomenon that appears impossible to avoid and difficult to manoeuvre. Global South countries such as India require the instruments of cyber space to improve governance delivery and achieve rapid progress. Ironically, these nations also struggle the most in securing their nationals from cyber threats. Western states such as the US have leveraged their power to install infrastructure for systematically gathering information that travels via global networks. Democracies like India have to confront tough questions on information flow and invasion of privacy.

As India aspires to accrue the benefits of cyber space by keeping its information pathways open, it becomes vulnerable to threats that travel alongside. As acknowledged capabilities and dedicated resources are being put in place by its adversaries, India faces danger from cyber space. Is the danger as real and acute as it appears? Is India prepared to mitigate them? While laws of armed conflict help maintain order in conventional kinetic attacks, cyber space is not fully covered by such laws. As a result, norms are being pushed by more advanced nations. Are these in India's interest? Can India guarantee constitutional civil liberties that are now becoming embedded in cyber space without compromising its security?

By engaging these questions, this paper brings the relation between cyber space and security (of humans and states) centre stage in contemporary debates on domestic politics, international affairs and strategy in India.

Introduction

Cyber space has spread to cover the entire world. World economy would crash if this medium is shut down or disturbed. Developing nations have found means for connectivity and equality in this new medium, which has become critical for their economy and governance delivery. However, the governance of internet, which is a central component of cyber space is contract driven by the US. While the medium is stated to be 'flat', its governance has major inequalities between the global North and the global South.

Cyber space has emerged as the fifth domain for warfare after land, sea, air and space (Economist, 2010). Cyber space is different from the other four domains as it is entirely manmade. While this medium has not brought in new actors, it has empowered existing ones differently. Cyber space has certain characteristics that make conventional approach to security difficult, some of these are: (a) cyber space transcends sovereign boundaries; (b) cyber space gives anonymity to the actor; and (c) operationally, cyber space empowers all actors, equally.

Threats can now travel without constraints of geographies, boundaries and time, thus posing newer challenges and demanding newer solutions. This has thrown new challenges to established norms of security as well as governance and society in general. This secular cyber space has made distances meaningless, and has disrupted power equations between the individual and state and inter-state.

India's Security Strategy and Practice

India does not have a declared security strategy document. Experts see two reasons for this: First is that India has been unable to produce a political consensus on national security issues and secondly that it has been unable to address the crucial issue of coordination required to formulate and address national security matters (Gupta, 2011: 1). However in practice, India has generally adopted defensive posture with an aim to protect its territorial integrity. India has not projected its power beyond a self-set limit of geographical area. Resilience and recovery have been the methods of handling internal challenges. In nuclear arena, India has stated policy of 'No First Use'. India's approach to security in cyber space, while being aligned with national security strategy, has to be different from that of conventional security. In order to clearly understand the challenges involved, the domain would be first explored, then cyber security issues discussed.

Origin of Internet, Privileged Role for the US

Cyber space, the domain of machine mediated communication between human beings, has come a long way. [2] Data communication between computers started as a lab tool for scientists to share information in an environment of trust. In the initial stage, US centric, stage defence R&D controlled this upcoming domain, later, civilian and commercial corporations were brought in. Subsequently, it spread to its allied countries, the global North and then to the South. This machine mediated communication web continues to penetrate deeper into our society and our lives—it is essentially a technologically driven domain. Development of internet, a critical component of cyber space, has been a US centric process and managed by a plethora of agencies. Some of these agencies are loosely structured groups with diffused leadership, others are commercial and a few are international organisations. Retaining first mover's advantage, the US dominates over technological development as well as management structures. [3]

In global North, specially the US, internet has evolved over the last few decades and spanned over a few generations of its citizens. In contrast, internet came to South as an evolved structure and is still seen as a young phenomenon. The disparity in internet penetration can be seen from International Telecom Union's (ITU) statistics for 2013, which shows that in global North countries, 78.4 percent of population use internet, while in the South that figure is only 31.2 percent (ITU, 2014). In countries like ours, during the initial stages, the government tapped this network of computers to better its accounting and delivery mechanisms as well as education systems. Only recently has its spread been driven by private individuals [As per latest ITU estimates percentage of population in India using internet has gone up from 0.53 percent in 2000 to 12.58 percent in 2013 (ITU, 2014)].

Role of Private Players and Lack of Security

After steering and managing the internet backbone for the initial 2 decades, US opened the field for private players in 1990s. The standards and structures for internet are discussed and decided by groups, largely made up of private players, through a system of 'request for comments' (RFC). These RFCs are almost always steered by a single or a group of large internet technology companies. The intention always has been to make internet acceptable to the largest number of stakeholders and enable easier communication. Due to this approach, internet has seen rates of growth never earlier witnessed in the history of humankind (Leiner et al., 1996).

The aim of private companies is to maximize revenue by endearing their product to largest number of buyers—Metcalfe's Law (Anderson, 2001). New systems and new features to existing systems are constantly being added by technology companies in this domain—the persistent quest for 'killer app'.

Functionality and security are two different aspects and often come at cost of one another. Hence, only the most essential security is taken into consideration at the time of designing functionality. Due to the diffused nature of this domain, each actor is responsible for its own security. [4]

Power of the Internet

This flat network is redefining relations between an individual and the state. The state, hereto considered all powerful, has started facing lots of probing questions and protests. This in a large measure is good for governance, but if overdone, it has the potential to induce instability. This is panning out in form of Arab spring in front of us. Nation-states have a reason to be anxious on this aspect and this is causing them to initiate measures to seek control over the cyber space.

The other facet of the flat network is that individuals now have the right to question the gap between policy and conduct of the state. This is playing out in form of 'Edward Snowden' phenomenon. Here, incidentally the affected party is the US that wields enormous cyber power, as will be covered later. This episode has also brought out the 'unflat' aspects of this flat world. It has exposed to public view, the resources and infrastructure employed by US, and the global North in general, to monitor and guide communication in the cyber space.

Importance of Internet for India

Internet as a medium for connectivity is important, especially so for the global South. India has connected to the world and now holds aspirations of becoming a global power, partly due to the knowledge economy it has developed around cyber space. Internet users in India are growing at the rate of more than 15 percent per annum and in 2013, 12.58 percent of Indians were internet users (ITU, 2014). [5] It is expected that by the end of 2015, number of internet users in India at 302 million, would be more than that in the US at 280 million. Internet driven activities contribute 4.1 percent of GDP in India (BCG, 2012: 8). The efforts have been directed to catching up in terms of 'functionality' in countries of the global South. The focus is now shifting to possible malevolent use of internet and thus cyber security.

Governance Delivery

Countries in the global South, in general, missed out on first round of progress whereby equality was attained within the societies of the North. Connectivity fostered by the internet has enabled these countries in the South to empower their populace and attain equality. This social progress is critically dependent on delivery of services and information through cyber space. Quality education in India is possible today at almost all locations thanks to this connectivity. Medical delivery is following a similar trajectory.

Indian IT service companies have a proven record and continue to attract large amount of business from more advanced countries. Indian economy has leveraged cyber technology to expand at a very rapid pace. From stock exchanges to banks to insurance to investments, everything is online today.

Power is ability of an actor to act and make others act as per its will. Power exercised through cyber space is cyber power. Neither is it a new form of power nor it brings along newer type of actors.

Cyber space is the newest domain where power is being exercised by nation-states and non-state actors. However, it is the nation-states that are important actors and in focus here. Four types of cyber power have been defined by D.J. Betz and Tim Stevens in 'Cyberspace and the State' (Stevens, 2011), based on Barnett and Duvall, 'Power in International Politics' as:

Direct Power: Power of an actor to get some act committed by another, normally an unwilling actor. A type of cyber crime through a virus known as 'crypto locker' is a case of use of direct power by the malevolent actor in making the target pay ransom for unlocking important information on his own machine.

Structural Power: Power that an actor derives from the structure of a relation, through which it is exercised. The power that aid-giver nation has on deciding the end-use of advanced system given to aid-receiver nation is an example of such power.

Institutional Power: Power need not be exercised directly; it can also be exercised through bilateral, multilateral or global institutions—the power of the US due to its contractual control of ICANN, ISOC and IANA.

Productive Power: Power of an actor to produce behaviour or discourse to its advantage. Cyber space in more conducive to exercising of this power through 'soft' means. Psyops used by US army email suggesting Iraqi troops to surrender prior to its invasion of Iraq is an example. Ability to continually define newer standards through R&D and participation in IETF by MNCs like CISCO in cyber space is also an example of productive power. Non-state actors in cyber space come to possess this type of power more frequently as compared to other domains.

The power of the strategic party is not due to cyber space, it is due to all the factors and environment combined that produce power for the strategic party—cyber space is one of the domains where it is exercised. A nation-state cannot become a cyber power without being powerful in conventional terms. Cyber space is domain for abstractions and virtualisations, whereas exercise of power needs to have some physical manifestation.

Power is exercised in a relation and towards an end-goal (Stevens, 2011). Malevolent power operates towards detriment of the target actor. Based on actor and the ends to which this power is operated, the threat event can be classified as cyber crime, cyber terrorism, cyber attack or cyber warfare (Oona A. Hathaway, 2012).

Cyber Crime: This is operation of cyber power by non-state actors towards another party with the intention of causing financial or any other loss in an illegal or unlawful manner

Cyber Terrorism: This is exercise of cyber power or threat thereof by a non-state actor with the intent to cause harm or intimidate general population for furtherance of some social, ideological, religious or political objective.

Cyber Attack: This is operation of cyber power by a state or non-state actor to undermine the functions of a computer network of the other party for a political or national security purpose.

Cyber Warfare: These are cyber attacks where effects are equivalent to an "armed attack", or such cyber attacks that occur in the context of armed conflict (Jenkins, 2005).

Cyber space does not recognize sovereign boundaries; security in this domain has different connotations as compared to conventional security. Cyber space affords anonymity and deniability, hence can be used by state and non-state actors alike to create disturbance in the networks of target state/actor. It is at times difficult for target actors to immediately detect cyber attack. When data from successive events is collated, analysed and the intent behind the events is understood, does the distinction between cyber crime and cyber warfare become clear. The differences between the two are the attacking actor and the intent—in cyber warfare the intent is political and is always driven by a state actor either directly or indirectly.

India is located in a very active neighbourhood, where newer capabilities are being constantly added. China has publically acknowledged the existence of a cyber security squad. Besides this, US periodically comes out with the news of existence of groups in China that attack US networks. India has also attributed some attack on its sites to groups in China. Groups such as 'Comment Crew' or PLA unit 61398 and 'Network Crack Program Hacker' group (or NCPH) are accused of sophisticated attacks on various governmental networks in the West.

Chinese groups are accused of commercial espionage, including theft of trade secrets, over prolonged period by Western, especially US companies. Various information security service providers credit Chinese with very advanced cyber penetration capabilities. India has been a victim of such cyber incidents triggered by the Chinese actors. China has a history of hiding behind non-state actors to carry out such attacks. In a low effect cyber attack on DRDO sites (just involving defacing some sites and attempting to steal some data) in 2012-13, a group known as 'NetTraveler' was suspected to be used by the Chinese government (The Hindu, 2013).

Hacker groups in Pakistan have always been attacking Indian websites, especially those belonging to governmental organisations like the Railways, BSNL, and BARC etc. These attacks generally tend to 'low end defacement of site' kind. However, of late, there has been an increase in the number of attacks as well as their sophistication. The main aim of these attacks is to bring down the site and redirect the surfer to a page where anti-India messages are posted. Due to the quantum of attacks, it is suspected that with mapping of such sites available with Pakistan, a sophisticated persistent attack can be launched against the Indian sites.

Response in terms of 'resilience and recovery' is not the most optimal option in cyber space. Hence, the concept of active defence has gained ground, wherein an effort is made to locate and neutralize the source of disturbance. This would require handling of situation by military experts and not just policing. Typical military handling is by escalation and response, and thus bringing war into this discussion.

Law of Kinetic Attack

Law of War (kinetic attack) as applicable to conventional war provides acceptable justification of initiating a war (jus ad bellum) in one part and the limits of acceptable wartime conduct (jus in Bello) in the second part. These laws are supplemented by various articles of the UN Charter. The recent report of the Group of Governmental Experts looking into information security aspects recommended that "international law, and in particular the Charter of the United Nations, is applicable and is essential to maintaining peace and stability and promoting an open, secure, peaceful and accessible ICT environment".

However, the following difficulties arise in applying the existing laws to cyber war:

1. Handling of attacks with no physical consequences.
2. When does cyber attack constitute armed attack or use of force? (Necessity)
3. How to distinguish between combatants, civilians directly participating in hostilities, civilians engaged in a continuous combat function, and protected civilians in the context of cyber attacks? (Distinction)
4. How does one decide on proportionality in cyber attacks? (Proportionality)
5. How does one decide on neutrality of a state in case of a cyber attack, especially in case where it appears to have originated from that state? (Neutrality)

Cyber Threat

"Our nation is at a grave risk of a cyber attack that could devastate the national psyche and economy more broadly than did the 9/11 attacks". *(Statement in a letter sent to President Bush by former White House adviser Richard Clarke and more than 50 top computer scientists, quoted in Fitzpatrick, 2003).*

Cyber attacks have neither fingerprints nor the smell of a gun powder. Cyber threat has been fascinating humans for some time now. For example, in the 1986 movie 'War Games', a teenager hacks his way into the computer that handles command and control for the US nuclear arsenal.

Categories of Threat: Cyber threat has been discussed at various levels in the last 25 odd years since we started living in this networked world. It is mostly at the technical level that these are grouped into different types of malicious programs. Here, we look at the semantic level and using Barry Buzan's concept of sectors of security; we examine how this threat can be categorised and discuss its relevance.

Military Threats (Threat to Existence): This is the gravest threat faced by a nation-state or humanity in general. There are two ways in which cyber space can be used for military action, firstly as a standalone and secondly as a force multiplier. Attacks originating and effecting assets only in cyber space are types of cyber attack, example is bringing down a server through a virus attack. Such types of attacks generally would not be very serious, as critical systems are complex and resilient by design hence can sustain such attacks. Cyber space has been classified as fifth domain of warfare after land, sea, air and space. Cyber space action can take place in conjunction with action in any other domain, thus enhancing the overall effectiveness of the action—this is very potent and can result in 'existential threat'. Example is Israel's air attack on Syrian Nuclear Reactor in 2007 (code named Operation Orchard) where Israeli F15 and F16 aircraft entered Syria and bombed its upcoming nuclear reactor in Deir ez-Zor region without being detected by Syrian Radars and Air Defence System (Fulghum, 2007).

Political Threat (Threat to Sovereignty): For the sake of simplicity, political threat is divided into two parts: threat to sovereignty and threat to institutions. Cyber space does not recognize boundaries of nation-states. Looking at the rapid pace of spread of cyber space across sovereign boundaries, it was termed as 'anti-sovereign' and claims were made that sovereignty as well as the idea of a nation-state were on wane. However, this has not happened and more importantly it is unlikely to happen. What has however happened due to rapid sharing of information is that the social, political as well as national order has altered and continues to happen even today. The image of primary power in sovereign state as controller of information flow has been shattered by this new democratization of information. This is perceived as a threat by a large number of political dispensations as has been the case of Hosni Mubarak in Egypt, Bashar-al-Asad in Syria; closer home, the same was witnessed during the 'Lokpal' movement of Shri Anna Hazare.

Political Threat (Threat to Institutions): 'Our way of life' exists because of institutions and structures developed over a period of time that ranges from simple delivery mechanism for essentials to sovereign institutions. If the trust these institutions enjoy, gets undermined, then there will be unrest in the society and 'our way of life' would be compromised. Cyber space has the potential to bring forth such disturbance or destruction into interaction between public institutions and general public through disruption of communication channels used there.

Societal Threat (Threat to Co-existence): Societies are dynamic structures that evolve in response to stimuli it receives from the environment and its constituents. With distances and time becoming meaningless due to cyber space, the stimuli travel across societies almost instantaneously. However, societies change at differing rates and direction—any effort in pushing through the changes would cause unrest. This is the chief threat that societies face from cyber space.

Economic Threat (Threat to Information): This is the primary threat in cyber space. As cyber space is a 'public' space, data is at risk once it is in such an open domain. The technical systems are so designed that confidentiality of user data is maintained, but like all technical systems, these can also fail. Online fraud and privacy attacks are manifestations of such failings. Hence, user, whether an individual or a nation-state needs to understand the risk of putting data onto cyber space and act accordingly.

Tools to Address or Mitigate the Threats

A nation-state can deploy tools at its disposal to guard against cyber threat as well as neutralize any attack that takes place. These tools are available for action at all the three layers: technical, syntactic and semantic. The emergence of threat is initially acknowledged, in case it persists and spreads to cover larger population in a given nation-state, it starts getting discussed. Some of the threats will be considered serious enough to be politicized and hence will have a designated policy response to tackle it. A very few will be converted to the 'existential' level where an emergency response is warranted. To an outsider, the threats that are converted to the existential level may seem to be totally unrelated to existence, however in target nation's discourses, it would occupy a primary place and consensus would rapidly emerge to adopt emergency measures.

Nation-states have three categories of tools to secure their cyber space:

1. Technical and physical security—measures to physically and electronically guard its assets from any damage.
2. Control through legal measures filtering out undesirable actors and actions.
3. Active defence or offensive counter measures—neutralizing threat before it can inflict damage on assets or after it has started its damaging activity.

It is essential that only in extreme situations threats should be allowed to progress to an 'existential' level where need for offensive counter measures and kinetic action arise. This can be done by politicizing issues early and controlling threats through sound policies/laws. Policies can be better designed only in cases where areas of influence of the nation-state are clearly understood and cyber security aligned with larger national security (Kuehl, 2009).

Map Areas Where Nation Can Influence

Nations are only actors equipped to act in a manner that mitigates military and political threats. The tools that a nation deploys depend on the power it has as well as the threat it is facing. In cyber space, the relation between developed countries and developing countries is that of a provider and a receiver of technology and hence the former has structural power that it can exercise over the latter. Also, the internet governing organisations give US, an unparalleled institutional power, while denying the same to most of the other nations. Direct power, could be used in extreme cases, in case a particular nation possesses such power. Productive power can be used by nations like India that have skill, technology and infrastructure to deliver positive results and shape public opinion. However, India needs to work towards acquiring or at least reducing disparity in structural power and institutional power in cyber space.

Two Main Approaches to Cyber Security

Cyber security is no longer exclusively the preserve of the engineer, the programmer or the system administrator, but has become the responsibility of the soldier, the politician and the diplomat too.

The rapid pace of development of internet can be attributed to relatively coherent groups of technical experts on various topics (Leiner et al., 1996). These groups included representatives from technology companies that were quick to market products and services on the finalized 'standards'. However, in such a setup, considerations of security and control were sidelined. Now that security issues are being discussed, two distinct approaches have emerged for handling the process, which are now discussed (Kleinwächter, Internet Governance Outlook, 2013).

Norms and Ends-based Approach: The US, where these internet governing structures have evolved and which can project power through the cyber space better than any other nation is pushing for continuation of same structures. 'World Summit on Information Society' held at Tunis, in November 2005 was able to conclude with a declaration only after it was agreed that US would retain control over ICANN. Led by the US, the global North is steering discourse towards two goals:

- Adoption of norms for cyber security and internet governance. The method of consultations being followed in the existing internet institutions like IETF is conducive to evolution of norms; hence norms that have larger appeal can be evolved—multi-stake holder approach. Norms can be formalized as either bilateral agreements or multilateral agreements, hence giving them political sanctity (Tim,

2011). This would also keep various international institutions like the UN out of this domain.

- Ends-based approach to cyber security. US argues that cyber space can be used only as a medium to carry out malicious activity. For such an activity, the end result if it is illegal under the existing laws should be tackled under those laws. Cyber security/cyber laws should focus on activity confined to cyber domain only. The opinion here is that, in case cyber laws are made applicable to activity that uses cyber space only as a means then such laws can be misused for censorship and other undemocratic suppression.

Rules and Means Approach: Countries like China and Russia, who are opposed to institutional power cantered around the US, are approaching the problem of cyber security and internet governance from a different view point. The structures of internet governance have evolved outside their areas of influence and do not adequately represent position of countries in the global South. The following is the alternative that is being proposed:

- Involvement of multilateral bodies like ITU in laying down rules for governance of internet and cyber space in general—multilateral approach. This will ensure primacy of sovereign political authority in each nation-state. Also, rules of engagement would be clearly defined and any deviation can be addressed within the established international regime.
- Cyber space is being used for propaganda and shaping of discourse that could be detrimental to the social setup in a nation-state. The international laws and rules need to be framed for cyber security that would ensure prohibition of use of cyber space as a means for such malicious activity.

Current Situation

Both these approaches have their merit and limitations. Some recent events like Wikileaks and Edward Snowden episode has brought forth the limitations to ends-based approach as charges disconnected with cyber activity carried out are being slapped on Julian Assange and Edward Snowden. Similarly, the exodus of people from the North-East as an aftermath of threat of violence in reaction to some images circulated among people of certain religion is pointer to limitation to ends-based approach.

On the other hand, attempted censoring of social media by Hosni Mubarak of Egypt brings to front the probability of misuse of means based approach. Similar censorship demanded by various political leaders at various times within our own country is also an example of the same limitations. In fact, at a recently concluded meeting of UN mandated Working Group on Enhanced Cooperation (WGEC), first signs of some consensus between two approaches is seen to be emerging (Kleinwächter, Enhanced Cooperation in Internet Governance: From Mystery to Clarity, 2013).

In global North, the recent exposure about role of NSA (Nicole Perlroth, 2013), has worked to break down the consensus about multi-stakeholder approach being pushed by the US. Some in the North have started talking about multilateral approach being pushed by China and Russia. In Geneva meeting of WGEC during November 2013, a hybrid of the two approaches seems to be evolving—multilateral multi-stakeholder approach.

Scenario in India

India has benefited from rapid spread of internet in the form of increased awareness levels and prosperity. Also, society is becoming more equal due to empowering effects of connectivity. Social networks are being used by various actors to steer opinions and pilot discussions. This is possible due to free and ubiquitous internet and hence India's interest in keeping it that way.

Cyber space and its tools are also used by malicious actors for propaganda. Recent cases of radicalization of youth of certain communities with an aim to motivate them to join ISIS in Syria were mostly carried out through internet. Earlier, morphed images were circulated using social networking application on mobile phones to instigate communal violence in U.P. and Delhi. These are examples of societal threat that travelled through the internet. As a nation-state is the only level at which such threats can be effectively tackled, India needs to have a handle to mitigate such threats, which in turn requires projection of power in cyber space.

Cyber security has to find a place on political front line for resources to be devoted in that direction. Speech acts indicate the kind of issues that are lined up for polity introspection (Cavelty, 2008). By that yardstick, cyber security or for that matter information technology itself does not figure anywhere in political statements so far. This issue found no mention in Indo-China joint statement during Chinese president's India visit and only a fleeting mention in Indo-US joint statement during US president's India visit. However, economic utility of IT was mentioned in both the statements. India has been a downstream state for IT industry, where technology developed elsewhere is put to use to enable service delivery and job creation. Efforts will have to be made to bring cyber security into our political discussions. It is only after that, the resources would be devoted to this important area which will bring in benefits of more representative internet and more secure cyber space to this country.

India's Cyber Security Initiatives

India's cyber security aims are incongruent with those of either the US or China/Russia. On one hand, India desires that internet should stay un-partitioned and on the other hand, it desires equitable distribution of resources and equal say in governance. Due to social setup and stage of its digital evolution, a rule based approach suits India's requirements better than norms based approach. Also, India has very mature and capable private sector engaged in delivery of world class services in cyber space and a vibrant civil society, both of which can assist India in achieving its cyber security goals.

India needs Multilateral approach but along with a definite role for private partners and civil society.

India has recently announced a National Cyber Security Strategy and formed some structures to address issues related to cyber security. The approach is largely focused on preventing cyber crime by strengthening resilience at the technical level. The strategy goals in non-technology areas are difficult to operationalize due to lack of clarity. For example, skill sets and end use of large number of cyber security professionals that this strategy aims for training is not clear. The strategy is following template of the US at superficial level by propping institutions with similar sounding names and broad mandate. No effort at linking India's capabilities and threats is apparent from this strategy document. Main reason for this is the lack of coherent policy in this domain.

India has acquired certain strengths in this domain and accrued economic benefits of the same. These strengths have largely been driven by private initiative and entrepreneurial zeal. Institution nurturing has not been seriously encouraged. In the field of cyber security, isolated capabilities have emerged in technical field with selective effort to link these by some sectorial agencies. India has no legal framework for cyber security; the field is governed by a law that is essentially an e-commerce enabling instrument that can at best handle economic threats in the cyber space. Efforts have been targeted towards preventing cyber crime, which requires a policing approach. Cyber attacks and cyber warfare have been left orphaned. Policy and international relations aspects of cyber security do not have any established forum and are being tackled by existing institutions on case to case basis without any broad guiding philosophy.

Power projection in cyber space is essential for a nation-state to reassure the users of their rights being protected. For this projection, the relevant power, based on the strengths need to be operationalized. India has been a downstream state as far as cyber technology is concerned; it has been largely catering to demands of large corporations in the West and producing services on their designs. All tools of production have been designed and mostly developed in the West. The standards for such development and acceptance of services have also been developed in the West.

Essentially, it is the labour intensive part of detailed designing, coding, testing and documentation that is done in India. Besides, India is one among few other such centres where such activities are being done. India enjoys certain competitive advantages, but it does not enjoy monopolistic powers. Besides, these are of commercial nature and cannot be easily converted to strategic advantages.

India is well poised to acquire and project productive power in cyber space. The most fundamental level it could be developed could be in the form of a public good distribution system in cyber space. This system could be targeted towards solving emergent problems or addressing unresolved issues efficiently and effectively. On the policy level, such institutions need to be seeded and nurtured. There have to be partnerships between private enterprises that have the requisite expertise and processes to deliver cyber systems on one hand and governmental agencies that bring in finance and long-term perspective on the other.

For this, the government needs to commit resources; this would be possible only when a policy is defined for cyber power and cyber security. Policy definition takes place after a subject repeatedly finds a place in public discourse; and gains importance. To start this sequence of activities, cyber security needs to be put into public debate by all the stakeholders and all those interested in its long-term utility.

Conclusion

Cyber space has evolved as the fifth domain for power projection by nation-states. Additionally, non-state actors have acquired unprecedented power in cyber space to disturb or destroy infrastructure in a target nation-state. India's conventional security approach may not be most optimal for securing cyber space. Though cyber space helps in flattening the world by offering similar opportunities to all irrespective of other factors, the powers that nation-states wield are not equal. India, though leading in providing information services does not wield adequate power that can be opertionalised. The areas where power can be exercised in cyber space by country like India are also limited.

India needs to make difficult choices to continue with their progress using cyber space while staying secure. A comprehensive and more thought out security policy rather than ad hoc responses would serve its cause better. It is necessary to carry out threat assessment to actually quantify the threat—what is under threat, from whom and how. This would lay out contours for its response and assigning of resources. Based on such threat assessment, a strategy would then evolve to tackle the threat. It is essential to have an escalation matrix—thus a simple cyber crime would be dealt differently as compared to cyber attack. This is similar to mechanism that exists in conventional security infrastructure where petty crime is handled by local police and cross border attack by defence forces. Cyber security strategy has to align with national security strategy as cyber space is just one of the domains where security of a nation can be threatened. One major difference between conventional security and cyber security is the dynamic nature of the domain itself. The strategy has to be capable of rapid execution and adaptation.

Endnotes

1. I am thankful to Dr. Sanjay Jha and Dr. Atul Mishra of Central University of Gujarat for their valuable comments on earlier drafts.
2. In "Cyberspace and The State: Toward A Strategy For Cyber-Power", David J. Betz and Timothy Stevens, describe cyber space thus: "...cyber space as a term is a mere 30 years old, cyber space as the metaphorical 'place' in which machine-mediated communications occur is more than a century old".
3. 'Internet Corporation for Assigned Names and Numbers' (ICANN) is responsible for allotting IP addresses and approving names for internet sites, is a corporation registered in California,

US. 'Internet Engineering Task Force' (IETF) is a loose body of experts that has ownership for standards on internet; it has almost 50 percent representatives from the US.

4. Tom Quiggin in his Occasional Paper: "Don't Call Us: Governments, Cyber Security, and Implications for the Private Sector", lists one of the problems as relatively low investment that software producers devote to improving the security of their product. Unlike providers of other mainstream products or services, software companies are rarely held financially liable for defects in their products.
5. While TRAI is listed as one of the sources for data at ITU site quoted here, TRAI site does not give data in this form; also internet connection figures quoted there are different. As depth of data at ITU site is more, it has been chosen.

References

Anderson, Ross (2001). "Why Information Security is Hard: An Economic Perspective", 17th Annual Computer Security Applications Conference, IEEE Computer Society.

BCG (2008), "The Internet Economy in the G-20 Economies", Boston Consulting Group.

Cavelty, Myriam Dunn (2008), "Cyber Security and Threat Politics", Oxon: Routledge.

DeiTy (2013), "National Cyber Security Policy", New Delhi: Department of Electronics and Information Technology, Government of India.

DSCI (2013), "DSCI Analysis of the National Cyber Security Policy, 2013", New Delhi: Data Security Council of India.

Economist (2010), "Cyber War: War in the Fifth Domain", *Economist*, July 1.

Fulghum, David A. (2007), "Why Syria's Air Defences Failed to Detect Israelis", October 3, available at: http://www.aviationweek.com.

Gupta, Arvind (2011), "A National Security Strategy Document for India", New Delhi: IDSA, October 20.

Jenkins, Cdr. Vida M Antolin (2005), "Defining Parameters of Cyber Warfare Operations", *Naval Law Review*, 51.

Kleinwächter, Wolfgang (2013), "Enhanced Cooperation in Internet Governance: From Mystery to Clarity?", November 12.

Kuehl, Dan (2009), "From Cyberspace to Cyber Power", in Stuart H.

Starr, Larry Wentz Franklin and D. Kramer (eds.), 'Cyber Power and National Security', National Defence University Press.

Nicole Perlroth, Jeff Larson and Scott Shane (2013), "US Web Spying: NSA Foils Much Internet Encryption", *The Times of India*, September 6.

Oona A. Hathaway, Rebecca Crootof, Philip Levitz, Haley Nix, Aileen Nowlan, William Perdue and Julia Spiegel (2012), "The Law of Cyber Attack", *California Law Review*, Vol. 100, No. 4, pp. 817-885.

Reserve Bank of India (2013), "Report on Trend and Progress of Banking in India: 2012-13", available at: http://www.rbi.org.in.

Stevens, David J. Betz and Tim (2011), "Cyberspace and the State", London: Routledge.

The Hindu (2013), "India Prime Target of Chinese Cyber Espionage", *The Hindu*: Chennai.

Tim, Maurer (2011), "Cyber Norm Emergence at the United Nations: An Analysis of the UN's Activities Regarding Cyber-security?", Cambridge: Belfer Centre Discussion Paper.

Index

Index